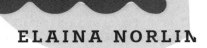

ELAINA NORLIN

The Six-Step Guide

to Library Worker Engagement

ALA Editions

Chicago | 2021

ELAINA NORLIN is the professional development Diversity, Equity, and Inclusion (DEI) coordinator for the Association of Southeastern Research Libraries. She is an accomplished teacher, technology and leadership development trainer, and writer with extensive leadership experience and a flair for public relations, organizational development, marketing, and persuasion and communications. The author of two books, she has delivered over seventy workshops, training sessions, presentations, and institutes both nationally and internationally on marketing, web usability design, facilitation, strategic influence, and conflict management.

Extensive effort has gone into ensuring the reliability of the information in this book; however, the publisher makes no warranty, express or implied, with respect to the material contained herein.

ISBN: 978-0-8389-4798-2 (paper)

Library of Congress Cataloging-in-Publication Data
Names: Norlin, Elaina, author.
Title: The six-step guide to library worker engagement / Elaina Norlin.
Description: Chicago : ALA Editions, 2021. | Includes bibliographical references and index. |
    Summary: "The book provides advice on how to enhance employee engagement and improve
    workplace culture"—Provided by publisher.
Identifiers: LCCN 2021000859 | ISBN 9780838947982 (paperback)
Subjects: LCSH: Library personnel management—United States. | Library administration—
    Employee participation—United States. | Library employees—United States—Attitudes. |
    Leadership—United States. | Library directors—United States—Interviews. | Librarians—
    United States—Interviews.
Classification: LCC Z678 .N66 2021 | DDC 023.0973—dc23
LC record available at https://lccn.loc.gov/2021000859

Book design by Alejandra Diaz in the Tisa Pro and Neusa Next Std typefaces.

♾ This paper meets the requirements of ANSI/NISO Z39.48-1992 (Permanence of Paper).
Printed in the United States of America

25 24 23 22 21   5 4 3 2 1

The Six-Step Guide to Library Worker Engagement

ALA Editions purchases fund advocacy, awareness, and accreditation programs for library professionals worldwide.

Contents

Preface

My original goal in writing this book was to identify the characteristics of outstanding workplaces in the corporate world and then see how those characteristics play out in library organizations. My focus was on solutions and potential frameworks with which to create great places to work. To accomplish this, I have read extensively on employee engagement research, along with spending time with management consultant experts both inside and outside the library field. This background research has helped me refocus my thinking and consultant work on what constitutes a healthy, engaged workplace, along with how to successfully integrate diversity, equity, and inclusion initiatives into an organization. This book is designed to create awareness and provide advice on how to change workplace culture.

I once thought that a successful workplace culture was simply one where people were happy. I soon learned that plenty of people can be unhappy at their workplace, but glad to have a paycheck and benefits, while contributing little to their organization's success. This concept is called "checked out," where employees find a comfortable place where they are doing just enough to get by or the bare minimum at work. This is significant because most people think that being "disengaged" means that people have simply stopped working, but in reality, they are still fulfilling their basic job responsibilities, but with very little excitement, passion, or energy. We all know someone in the organization who is disengaged at work, and you even may have experienced this disengagement yourself. I know that I have been disengaged in the past and did not realize or understand what happened but the spark was gone at work, and eventually I resigned when I had found another job. Because disengagement is so prevalent in organizations, there are many researchers who study employee engagement and its direct correlation between productivity, creativity, and innovation. Engaged employees feel that their unique talents, skills, and abilities are valued and respected within the organization and that their work makes a difference. An engaged workforce propels creativity, innovation, and a healthier work culture. Organizations that cultivate employee engagement not only perform well, but in many cases they outperform their competitors.

The gold standard for employee engagement research is Gallup, the famous polling company. Every few years Gallup produces the *State of the American Workplace* (*SOAW*) report, which almost every major publication cites for data on workplace culture. Gallup has been conducting this research for well over thirty years, and the results have remained consistent. According to the 2019 report, over 70 percent of employees are disengaged at work (Gallup 2019). In terms of employee retention, more than 50 percent of employees are actively looking for a new job by reviewing job ads, engaging recruiters, or networking on sites like LinkedIn. Gallup distinguishes between employees who are "actively engaged" (loyal and productive), "not engaged" (average performers), and "actively disengaged" (checked out). If the percentage of people who are disengaged is over 60 percent, then the organization is moving toward a dysfunctional, static, or stagnant work climate.

Corporations have been studying and experimenting with employee engagement strategies in order to attract talent and improve retention. A revolving door out of a company hurts both its bottom line and its reputation. Companies are looking beyond pay and perks as they compete for talent. New trends include flexible schedules, remote work, coaching instead of supervising, more consistent feedback, recognition, and a more open, inclusive, and diverse environment. Research validates that employees young and old tend to favor companies which have programs that give back to the community. Employees who have the best experiences at work feel connected, feel a strong sense of purpose, receive recognition for their individual talents and contributions, and believe that their workplace is moving forward in a positive direction.

Great Place to Work is a global research and consulting firm that is known for quantifying the employee experience. The firm is the assessment arm for the annual *Fortune* 100 Best Companies to Work For list. I started my research by studying companies on the Great Place to Work certification list that were known for employee engagement initiatives. Great Place to Work representatives helped me settle on the areas of concentration for this book and recommended several companies for further research. I studied these companies and contacted a few employees for their input.

After talking to representatives at Great Place to Work and Gallup and doing some general research, I broke down my employee engagement research into six categories. Once I decided on the categories, I went back to the experts for verification and to see if I was on the right track. Each chapter in this book addresses one of these categories, and I have been intentional in their sequence:

- Leadership and management
- Trust
- Recognition and praise
- Feedback and performance evaluation
- Teamwork and collaboration
- Diversity, equity, and inclusion

As I narrowed my focus and looked at library organizations, I have relied heavily on firsthand accounts from library managers and workers. My original intent was to focus solely on success stories in libraries. I envisioned a book that would be a sort of "Chicken Soup for the Soul for Libraries," full of feel-good stories from libraries that are transforming their culture.

However, after putting out the call for "success stories" from the field, something unexpected happened; the success stories were fewer than I had hoped. Instead of success stories, I received tragic stories from people who felt lonely, isolated, and traumatized at work. Some of these people are still in their organization trying to figure out ways to cope. Others are actively looking for another job. Others have left the profession altogether with no plans to return. Many of the people who told these disheartening stories requested anonymity. I have included some of their stories in this book, along with a few success stories as well. The stories are narrated either by the tellers themselves or by me, based on my personal conversations with the tellers.

Another major component of this book are the question-and-answer interviews placed at the end of each chapter. These interviews are with successful library managers and administrators who are taking steps to improve their workplace culture. My introductions to the interviews are partly based on the site visits and personal observations I made at their libraries.

In the interviews, I asked my subjects questions about the six themes that lead to employee engagement. I present these interviews where I see a connection to the chapter theme, but the interviews are broader in scope. They provide living examples of how organizations have approached employee engagement.

REFERENCE

Gallup. 2019. "Engage Your Employees to See High Performance and Innovation." Gallup. January 9. www.gallup.com/workplace/229424/employee-engagement .aspx.

Acknowledgments

This book was an amazing journey, and I want to take time to thank the people who came along for the ride.

First, I want to thank all the people who contributed through interviews, site visits, and multiple phone calls. Some of these people needed to be off the record, but they were so brave and honest, and they provided insight into the engagement (and in many cases the lack of engagement) in their organization. For the individuals who not only took my phone calls but were willing to answer my questions for this book, I would like to offer my personal thanks:

Theresa Byrd is not only a "leadership whisperer" but also an amazing mentor.

Nancy Kirkpatrick came highly recommended for her trust work, and she delivered in spades.

Consuella Askew is not only a great boss but an awesome friend.

Alexia Hudson-Ward, who I met twenty years ago and knew she was going places . . . and I was right!

Jamar Rahming, whose leadership style is straightforward and effective. I enjoyed the simplicity of our conversations.

Ashley Rosener, whose work on "appreciative inquiry" may open up many opportunities for successful Diversity, Equity, and Inclusion (DEI) initiatives.

Doug Crane was pleasant to talk to and provided amazing recommendations that really opened up my work.

Pamela Espinosa de los Monteros and Sandra Aya Enimil were excellent at combining DEI initiatives with great teamwork.

Stephanie Case and Hillary Ostlund, thank you for restoring my positive faith in organizations with your incredible work.

Mary Jo Finch, thank you for your wisdom, insight, and pioneering work in creating antifragile environments.

Alyssa Jocson Porter and Lynn Kanne taught me the value of compassionate problem-solving and teamwork, and showed me their low-key, successful approach to creating a diverse organizational environment.

For site visits, a special thank-you to the Mandel Public Library (of West Palm Beach) and the Richland County Library (of Columbus, South Carolina). The hospitality you showed me, along with your positive energy and healthy work spaces, have been an inspiration.

For the ALA Editorial Board, thanks for your patience, with a special shout-out to *Patrick Hogan*, who took my random thoughts and ideas and challenged me by pushing me harder to find my own unique voice.

Next, a special thank-you to my family and friends, who propped me up at times of exhaustion, when I wanted to give up on the research. *Sam Morrison, Pam Adams,* and *Julie Hunter*, I will always value your mentorship, guidance, and unending support. To my former AARLCC staff and my former branch managers, *Michael, Marlene, Michelle, Tim, Maribel,* and *Joan*, I miss you much, and thanks for showing me necessary lessons along the way. I learned so much from you, and this book would not be possible without your presence. *Audrey Ljung* . . . love you much . . . you picked me up when I felt down, and you always make me feel like a superstar. *LaVonna,* thank you for challenging my thoughts and ideas, for pushing me when I was stuck, and for being a true-blue friend. The keeper of the status quo will always be your quote. *Lorisa,* thank you for keeping me laughing and for always seeing the glass half full. *Mom, Charles,* and *Lisa*, I love you all to pieces; thank you for being the loving family members everyone needs to have in their life.

Finally, to *Ithan Payne*, I would not have made it without you. Thanks for being my constant cheerleader, confidant, best hugger, best chef, and the ride-and-die person through both good times and bad. Love you always.

Leadership and Management

I measure my own success as a leader by
how well the people who work for me succeed.
—MARIA SHI

"I want to be the new museum director because I enjoy having the power to control others instead of being controlled." I looked up from my reading glasses at the person answering the question. I had been invited to serve on a search committee for a new museum director, and the interview question was about his leadership style. Why would someone answer that they need to control others as an answer to their leadership style? Overall, the candidate's qualifications were impressive, and he was very charming, but this was not his first "power and control" answer in the interview, and in my opinion, it was a major red flag. I was not alone in my assessment, and after the interview, several other search committee members raised the alarm to the museum board. The museum board members disagreed with our findings and thought the candidate's confident "take no prisoners attitude" was exactly what the museum needed to turn the place around. Two years later, this same museum board voted unanimously to fire the director in a vote of no confidence. This same "power and control" museum director had terrorized the museum staff members, alienated key donors, and ultimately caused a noticeable dip in museum attendance. The museum director did not leave quietly, and after a very public breakup that was covered on the news and radio, the museum was scrambling to repair the damage.

● ● ● ● ● ●

The road to employee engagement and a healthy workplace always starts and ends with good management. Gallup research consistently find that companies which have solid leadership always outperform their competition in creativity, innovation, low absenteeism, and low turnover (Crowley 2015). But how does an organization build the "right leadership team"? How do we select the best manager/supervisor/director for a position? This chapter is going to look at why libraries and other cultural heritage institutions are falling short at selecting good leadership and will suggest how to develop better recruitment strategies moving forward.

EMPLOYEE ENGAGEMENT

When I started interviewing people about their workplace culture, almost everyone had a terrible boss or horrible management story. Narcissistic bosses dressing people down in meetings. Micromanaging leaders who have employees write daily and sometimes hourly reports during the pandemic. A supervisor who stopped talking to his employees and gave them the "silent treatment" for three months until the staff members threatened to get a lawyer. An inflexible boss who turns down or ignores every new idea or project. A management team that fired five employees with an all-staff message a few days before the Christmas holiday. A cruel boss who laughed after berating a staff member until she broke down and cried during a staff meeting. For every one of these stories, the incidents were relayed like they had happened yesterday, and the incidents themselves left invisible scars of mistrust and disharmony in the organization.

However, when I turned the tables and asked interviewees what they thought great management would look like, it took people longer to reflect. After some thought, employees said they wanted managers to demonstrate how their work performance directly contributes to the success of the organization. Managers who create a sense of belonging for everyone in the organization regardless of the hierarchy within the organization. Managers who are open and flexible, and who encourage new and exciting ideas and allow people to fail forward. Leadership that celebrates accomplishments both large and small so that everyone feels they are part of a successful team. A management team that truly advocates for the staff and always has their best interests at heart. Managers who truly value diverse perspectives and lead with empathy, compassion, and kindness. Do we have any leaders who live up to these expectations? Of course we do, and there are wonderful leaders all over the world who are making a difference. The problem is that trying to pick an empathetic, compassionate leader who can inspire and motivate employees can often feel like a roll of the dice. So, how can we begin to move toward a healthier work environment by hiring good, talented managers? Before we consider this question, let's talk about whether anyone can become a leader or a manager.

ARE LEADERS BORN OR MADE?

Can anyone be taught to be a great manager with the right training? Does everyone have the right talent and is it really just a matter of timing and opportunity? A few years ago I created the "Are Leaders Born or Made?" workshop, which resulted in lively and informative conversations on this subject. During the workshop, we developed a list of things that would happen to an organization if there was great management. Then we looked at what traits, skills, and abilities are needed to be a great manager. Then we looked at various leadership, supervisory, and management job ads to determine the gap between what is needed for great management and how organizations actually recruit new managerial talent. Finally, I asked the million-dollar question: could their organization's current administration meet these "great leadership" expectations through training, coaching, and consulting? There were always a few participants who said yes, but most people in the workshop thought that it could not be accomplished. What does the research say?

Gallup research studies conclude that only 30 percent of the total workforce has what it takes to be a great leader. Other experts state that companies and organizations end up spending more money and time trying to fix bad leadership than in hiring the right leaders in the first place. "Spending the extra time and determining what skills are needed to positively move the organization forward eliminates the roll of the dice" (Chamorro-Premuzic 2017). "People skills" are very important in a successful manager. However, when you take a critical look at most job descriptions that require "people management," this kind of supervisory skill tends to be a throwaway line when compared to the quest for applicants with years of experience, impressive subject expertise, or professional recognition. Although the latter are all wonderful traits, they are not good indicators that a person can motivate, inspire, coach, and develop staff members.

For me, I was initially in the camp that anyone could be a good manager; they just needed the right training. I had personally taken several leadership trainings and participated in several management institutes before becoming a regional manager. However, after becoming a regional manager, what I observed is that some people are natural born leaders, some work hard to become better managers, and some should not even be managing potted plants. This did not mean that the bad managers were bad employees; they just did not have the "people management" gene.

To get an outsider's point of view, I sat down with a successful management consultant whose flourishing business is providing coaching and training for dysfunctional organizations. She said that she concluded years ago that natural leaders are born, not made, but saying this to clients is always bad for business. Her theory is that it's very hard to train or mentor people to become empathetic, compassionate, flexible, adaptable, and transparent. Because it's difficult and most organizations do a lousy job picking the right managers, she has stayed busy for over twenty-five years. She said the secret to her long-term success is her ability to quickly identify the emerging leader who is usually already working in the organization but is ignored by management. The best leaders are not the narcissistic ones who are consumed by ambition and are jumping up and down touting their own accomplishments. The best leaders are ones who people gravitate toward because they genuinely like people—the ones who are eternally positive and who know how to bring people together to resolve conflicts. Sadly, the consultant said that these people are often overlooked, even though they have the strongest foundation for leadership training.

From my experience, I tend to agree that some people are natural leaders, some can be trained, and some should pursue other promotional opportunities altogether. For me, I tell people all the time that I would make a horrible analyst because it does not suit my natural and unique talent and skills. However, if someone paid me good money and excellent benefits, could I do it in a pinch? The answer is yes. But should someone pick me? Well, the short answer would be that they would be better off with someone else who has the natural talent and aptitude for the analyst position. However, if I was truly motivated to become an analyst and I made a commitment to be the best analyst I can, then I have a better chance than just taking the job for a paycheck.

One senior manager told me off the record that he hated the "people" stuff but had a growing family at home and needed the additional income. During my "Are Leaders Born or Made?" training, I commonly ask participants a hypothetical question about managers getting the same pay and perks but eliminating all the "people stuff"; typically, about three-quarters of the participants raise their hands for that deal. These managers are not alone; Gallup states that 45 percent of higher-level executives are disengaged and only 29 percent of managers are engaged at work (Runyon 2017). If managers are not inspired and motivated on the job but don't want to let go of their pay and perks, how can they inspire their employees?

Before we address this, in the "Are Leaders Born or Made?" workshop we did address the elephant in the room. There were many people who were upset that not everyone could be a leader as this is usually the only avenue for career advancement. Many managers secretly hated their supervisory work, but they needed the money, or they were ambitious, or they wanted more independence and freedom. And to tell the truth, most organizations have only limited career promotion options that do *not* require supervising someone. To encourage employee engagement, some companies have explored other position titles (coordinators, project managers, project directors), along with financial incentives and promotional opportunities, which allow people to advance without being forced into people management. Toward the end of the workshop, the participants spent some time exploring these non-supervisory promotional options and how to make them a reality. Almost everyone agreed that providing more avenues to take the lead while leaving the "people management" to individuals who naturally shine in this area is always a win for an organization.

RECRUITMENT MISTAKES

Gallup had a controversial research study showing that companies fail to select the right talent for the job 82 percent of the time (Beck and Harter 2019). This fact, combined with the fact that only 30 percent of the workforce are more naturally inclined to leadership, means that spending some extra time on recruitment and the search process is needed. Where do traditional management searches go wrong? The first place to look is the job description and the recruitment materials. When you talk to people about what they're looking for when they're creating a job description for a position, the eight skills/abilities, personal traits, and qualifications in the list below always seem to rise to the top.

Here are some of the traditional skills/abilities, traits, and qualifications that organizations use to select a manager or supervisor:

1. Expertise/technical skills
2. Years of experience
3. Desire to get things right/perfect
4. Ability to discipline, fire, or manage "bad employees"
5. Previous supervisory experience
6. Ivy League education/Ivy League career
7. Outcomes, accomplishments, and professional reputation
8. Swagger, personality, confidence

On the surface, there is nothing wrong with this list. However, when you look at what makes a good manager or great leader, none of these qualifications guarantee success. In most cases, this is where the softer skills—skills involving the "people stuff"—come into play. Soft skills are the "intangible" qualities possessed by great leaders that make working for them so special. From my years of doing this exercise, the abilities listed below are what come to the top when we consider what people are truly looking for in a good leader.

Leaders should have the ability to:

1. Genuinely connect with others who may approach life and work differently. (*Social Intelligence*)
2. Deliver both good news and bad news. Can see both sides of an argument. Can make the tough decisions on behalf of the organization. (*Diplomatic*)

3. Encourage different points of view and change or modify plans as needed. Open to making mistakes and growing as a team. (*Flexible*)
4. Support individual goals by removing potential obstacles and setbacks along the way. (*Strategic Thinker*)
5. Take a step back and see the problem or concern from another person's point of view. How would I feel if this were happening to me? (*Compassion*)
6. Provide staff with their undivided attention during formal and informal conversations. Create opportunities for two-way communication. (*Active Listening*)
7. Take ownership and responsibility, admit mistakes, and recognize that they do not have all the answers. (*Personal Accountability*)
8. Stand up for their team and fight for equity, work-life balance, and equal opportunities. (*Advocate*)
9. Practice what they preach, and demonstrate honesty, transparency, trustworthiness, and reliability. (*Integrity*)

RECRUITING LEADERS AND MANAGERS

So, the next question is, if we are doing the management recruitment searches ineffectively, what are some strategies to revise the search process?

1. *Develop a leadership vison/statement.* This leadership statement/vision/philosophy should be created for the entire organization. The organization should come together and brainstorm what is needed in every department within the organization. From there, the organization should work on a leadership vision that should be implemented at all levels for continuity. Otherwise, the employees and staff will have vastly different experiences from department to department, where one area loves working for the organization and another department feels left out and unlucky. Once you have the leadership vision, that is what is added to the job recruitment documents so that candidates know up front the work expectations.
2. *During the job screening and job interview, make sure there is the right balance between questions to ascertain the candidate's competence and questions to ascertain soft skills.* This goes for both the prescreening interview and the selection interview. Once the organization

determines what it is looking for, the search committee can devise selection questions that will match the new qualifications. So, instead of eight or nine questions to probe the applicant's technical expertise, professional recognition, and years of experience, the committee has some questions on skills and expertise, and others to determine the applicant's empathy, compassion, flexibility, integrity, active listening, advocacy, and personal accountability.

3. *During the selection interview, listen closely for inflexibility, controlling tendencies, and self-absorbed tendencies.* In some cases, the wrong person will be obvious—like the museum director who wanted power to control (and to eventually terrorize) his staff members. At other times, it will require listening very closely to see if the person spends too much time talking only about themselves and their accomplishments, or appears inflexible, indifferent, or uninterested in the people management part of the job.

4. *Watch out for potential managers who lean toward perfectionism tendencies.* It cannot be stressed enough that perfectionism and inflexibility discourage cultivating a diverse workforce. Individuals with these traits are tempting picks because on the surface they appear to have high standards, are hardworking, are never satisfied, and are always pushing for a better product or outcome. However, when it comes to people management, they rarely recognize and praise their employees for jobs well done, they rarely take risks for fear of failure, and they reward assimilation instead of agility. Perfectionism can also cause some managers to have trouble delegating, to take on too much work, and to maintain a constant sense of urgency without much self-reflection.

Last year, I was recruited to apply for a position as a public library director. During the selection interview, I quickly noticed that five out of the nine questions were about how I disciplined, fired, or reprimanded "unruly" staff. When I casually mentioned to the selection committee that over 50 percent of the questions focused on punishment and penalty, I received cold stares and an eventual scolding that these were standard executive management questions. As you can imagine, I withdrew my candidacy as soon I returned home. Later, I found out through a mutual friend that the organization was suffering from low morale and trust issues and constant grievances from disgruntled staff. I told my friend that I was not surprised because the questions an organization selects can tell you a lot about that institution. So, make sure you take time to review your selection questions and what a potential candidate would conclude about your organization.

STRESS AND EMOTIONS AT WORK: CONFLICT RESOLUTION

Being able to manage stress and complex emotions at work, along with leading through positive reinforcement (addressed in the next section), are foundational skills that every manager should have at their disposal. When it comes to stress, almost every manager and supervisor must diffuse conflict, hurt feelings, and sometimes battles in the workplace. Managers who avoid conflict and ignore problems may think that ignorance is bliss, but tension and strife in the workplace can increase the stress level for everyone. Stress and conflict can make people lose focus, can decrease creativity and innovation, and can even make people want to leave their jobs. What current research has found is that people are more on edge at work nowadays, and the tensions between staff and team leaders are at an all-time high.

The following story is about a friend who was reentering the workplace. She is a tax accountant who started her career at a prestigious accounting firm with excellent pay and benefits. Within a few months, her dream job turned into a nightmare due to a toxic and sadistic boss, overly competitive colleagues, and grueling, thankless work. After spending two years fighting with the company—which left her alienated from everyone—she finally walked out without securing another position. Instead, she worked as an independent consultant for twelve years, but she never forgot the nightmare that her dream job had turned out to be. Fast forward to the present, where life changes forced her to consider going back to a corporate job to pay some outstanding medical bills. Because she had never resolved the pain from her initial corporate experience, she approached work understandably guarded and reserved. My friend was quick to start a fight, and she wrote meticulous notes about these interactions; moreover, she let people know that she kept these notes in folders in case she needed to seek legal action. Luckily, her manager noticed that she turned in excellent work, and people liked her but could sense some past trauma that was stopping her from trusting her new organization. So, the manager approached her, inquired about her past work experiences, and let her know that this organization was different and that they would work together to rebuild her trust in the organization and her new colleagues. My friend was a little resistant at first, but in time she came to trust the manager, and she began to see how her previous pain was showing up at the new job. With her manager's guidance, compassion, and positive reinforcement, my friend gradually began to let her guard down, which enabled her to enjoy both her job and her team members. Today, she loves her corporate job, her great pay, and her supportive boss, and she feels lucky that she selected a better option this time around.

The reason I mention this story is that every employee has what I call an "invisible bag" that they bring to work. In this bag are their life stories, the good times, the bad times, and any painful wounds or experiences that may or may not have healed. We have all observed people who are just fine during peaceful times but who become quite different when exposed to stress, high emotions, and conflict. There are some things we can predict in terms of triggers, but as in the case of my friend, she didn't see how her own actions were playing a part in creating workplace stress. In this case, her manager confronted the behavior and showed empathy and compassion, but expected my friend to improve the behavior. As she began to realize that the manager had her best interests at heart, she was able to open up and become a better team member. Being compassionate and empathetic doesn't mean that a manager should ignore conflicts in the workplace. Even the best manager—one who is normally calm and reasonable—can quickly turn agitated and unreasonable. Overall, for new managers, I recommend that the organization spend some time investing in conflict management and conflict resolution training and workshops so there are agreed-upon strategies on how to resolve problems in the organization.

PERFORMANCE MANAGEMENT

To obtain measurably superior results in the workplace, managers must understand why people behave as they do with the same depth that a rocket scientist understands gravity. (Daniels 2016)

When I first became a library director and regional manager, I was sent to standard, mandatory training classes. I noticed one thing right away; the county system spent a considerable amount of time going over the "progressive discipline" model. This model starts with a talk and, if the behavior does not get better, can end with dismissal. It is based on the premise that people want to avoid punishment, so they will adjust their behavior to avoid future negative consequences that could lead to their dismissal. This model appeared logical, but something did not feel right. Although most managers used progressive discipline, this tool rarely improved work performance, and in fact it often led to disengagement, grievances, and constant conflict. On the other side of the equation, one of the branch managers in my region never had any problems with his staff. While other managers spent much of their time in grievance hearings and writing expectation memos, this manager had happy employees, high productivity, and hardly any progressive discipline memos. What was his secret? I sat down with this very mild-mannered branch manager, and he said something that forever changed my perspective. He calmly told me: "I just expect the best out of my employees and praise them for their potential instead of their faults." I quickly remembered his staff evaluations, and they were all glowing, to the point that I secretly thought he was embellishing a bit. He admitted that his praises were not always 100 percent true, but by expecting the best from them, his staff almost always rose to the occasion.

So, why did this manager produce better results than the tried-and-true methods of progressive discipline? Why did "accountability and the constant threat of discipline" backfire in terms of employee engagement? It was not until I started my research that I came across a book that finally answered all of my questions. I will summarize some of its key points, but I highly recommend that you buy a copy of the book as a reference. The book is *Bringing Out the Best in People: How to Apply the Astonishing Power of Positive Reinforcement*, 3rd edition, by Aubrey Daniels.

In the book, Daniels looks at over eighty years of studies that focus on human behavior in the workplace. The application of the results of these scientific behavioral findings is called "performance management." It is performance management that teaches managers how to influence their employees' behavior. When it comes to behavioral analysis, Daniels spends most of the book talking about the behavioral consequences of *positive reinforcement* and *negative reinforcement* as these relate to employee engagement. The two consequences that increase behavior are positive and negative reinforcement. The two consequences that decrease behavior are punishment and penalty.

Inducing Behavioral Change: Positive and Negative Reinforcement

One of the things that was new to me is that both positive and negative reinforcement can motivate and encourage employees to change their behavior.

As already stated, *positive reinforcement* rewards the employee for adopting behavior that is desired by management. These rewards can be tangible ones like a bonus or a gift card to intangible ones like a pat on the back or a thank-you note. The theory is that if you reward someone for displaying behaviors that are likable, productive, and positive, that behavior is likely to be repeated. Positive reinforcement has been found to be one of *the most effective ways* to induce changes in behavior.

Example: Hayley has been late turning in her monthly reports. The manager sets up weekly meetings and praises Hayley for accomplishing smaller goals toward completing the monthly report on time. Once Hayley turns in her report on time, the manager sends a quick handwritten note congratulating her. Hayley, who enjoys the recognition and praise, works harder to get her monthly reports in on time.

Negative reinforcement motivates employees to perform better by confronting them with unpleasant consequences if they don't change their behavior for the better. Employees change their behavior to avoid negative consequences that they won't like. Negative reinforcement can be effective in changing behavior, but it is not as effective as positive reinforcement.

Example: Hayley has been late turning in her monthly reports. The manager sets up weekly meetings and complains and criticizes Hayley for not meeting expectations. Hayley, who does not like the complaints and the criticism, works harder to get her reports in on time. The manager, seeing that the work is being sent in on time, stops criticizing and complaining. Hayley is relieved and will work harder to get the report in on time to avoid the negative consequences.

Extinction is where there is no reinforcement (either positive or negative). Not addressing the negative behavior in the workplace allows that behavior to continue, which does not benefit the employee. Or it can cause disengagement because the employee is not receiving direction or guidance on management's expectations of the employee's work or job performance.

Example: Hayley has been late turning in her monthly reports. Her manager, not wanting to make waves, ignores this failing and works around the late report. Because the behavior is not being addressed, Hayley continues to be late with her monthly reports.

The final thing to note is that implementing more positive reinforcement in the organization requires additional work, and the organization may not see immediate results. But in the long run, it's worth the effort. Looking back at the branch manager who created a high morale/high productivity environment, it must have taken time for him to build trust and mutual esteem, but the ultimate outcome was highly positive, and it came from his dedication to positive reinforcement.

There are also cases where negative reinforcement is needed when serious infractions occur, but to turn a negative behavior into a positive one over the long term, it is always better to follow up with positive reinforcement.

Example: Hayley blows off an important assignment, which almost derails a major team project. Hayley is removed from the project (negative reinforcement) until she catches up with her work and can be an active member of the team. After some time, Hayley is able to rejoin the team. During the next assignment, Hayley turns in her part of the project before the deadline. The team manager sends Hayley a quick message thanking her for turning in the work on time and noting how much it meant for the entire project (positive reinforcement). Hayley is glad she is positively making a difference and is more committed to doing her fair share of the work.

Inducing Behavioral Change: Punishment and Penalty

There are two other ways to induce changes in behavior: *punishment* and *penalty*. Both of these methods are used to induce people to *unlearn* or stop practicing behaviors that are not desired or wanted by management. Both methods involve the imposition of negative or unfavorable consequences to discourage a specific behavior. Punishment and penalty in the workplace have the immediate effect of correcting the employee's behavior. The employee quickly understands specific work expectations and what could happen if the person continues the infraction. The proponents of punishment and penalty say that it increases accountability and personal responsibility.

Example: Hayley was running ten minutes late for work every day. The manager calls her into the office and tells her that if she doesn't report for work on time in the future, this infraction could ultimately lead to her dismissal. Hayley, afraid of losing her job, comes into work on time the next day and continues to do so thereafter.

Because penalties and punishments do produce immediate results and can speedily correct unwanted behavior, work organizations continue to use these forms as a motivational tool. At my former job, punishment and penalty served as a foundation for progressive discipline. Today's "cancel culture" is rooted in punishment and penalty. So, what is the problem with this approach?

The problem is that a steady dose of punishment and penalty can result in diminished creativity and innovation because employees are afraid of making mistakes, owning up to mistakes, or doing anything that may lead to an unfavorable reaction from management. And when there is too much punishment and penalty, you tend to hear words like "fear" and "intimidation," "hostile," "controlling," and "low morale." The way to remedy this is by using penalty and punishment only for serious infractions and, after they have been used, following up with positive reinforcement over the long term if the employee mends their ways.

Example: Hayley started an angry verbal altercation with a customer, and it was clear that she was in the wrong; a formal complaint was written. Her supervisor calls a meeting with her, explains the seriousness of the altercation, and instructs Hayley to take a customer service class and an anger management class. The supervisor also informs Hayley that any further infractions will result in a performance expectation letter (punishment and penalty). Hayley takes both classes, and the supervisor notices that she is clearly providing better service to patrons now. The supervisor brings Hayley back into the office, thanks her for the positive change at the customer service desk, and remarks that she is excited about Hayley's progress (positive reinforcement). Hayley knows that she made a mistake, has made the desired adjustments in her behavior, and is gratified that her current behavior is being positively rewarded at work, which encourages repeat outcomes for the future.

LEADERSHIP AND MANAGEMENT: RECOMMENDATIONS

- When recruiting new leaders and managers, make sure that the organization has a leadership vision or philosophy on how it wants them to lead the institution. This vision should be created with input from all the staff members through a facilitation or an outside consultant. From there, this leadership vision becomes the work expectations that are added to the recruitment package and are the standard for all managers.

- Good leaders can be made, but in many cases, it will require training, coaching, mentoring, and a willingness to change and work hard. However, the organization would do better picking leaders who have the needed soft skills and creating other, non-supervisory leadership opportunities for superstar employees who don't have the "people management" gene.

- Invest in a skill assessment tool(s) to evaluate the natural talents within the organization. There might be someone already in the organization who has the necessary soft skills and can be promoted and trained to be a good leader.

- Read more about behavioral analysis and how to motivate employees at work. It is crucially important to know how actions, policies, and procedures are directly and indirectly influencing behavior. Make sure that the policies and procedures are skewed more toward positive reinforcement—and in some cases, negative reinforcement—rather than penalty and punishment, which in larger doses lower both employee morale and engagement.

- Invest in some conflict management tools to handle unexpected stress in the organization. Spend some time as an organization to develop a multitude of strategies to resolve conflict.

INTERVIEW WITH
Theresa S. Byrd, Dean of the University Library

Theresa S. Byrd has been known as a library leader for over thirty years. When I was asking for recommendations on who to talk to about leadership, over fifteen people insisted that I talk to Theresa. And when one of her own staff members told me that she was the right person for this chapter, I was sold.

Theresa is the dean of the University Library at the University of San Diego. She is best known for developing the Association of College and Research Libraries' Dr. E. J. Josey Spectrum Scholar Mentor Program from 2002 to 2007. This program recruits experienced academic and research librarians to serve as mentors to library school students. The program is paired with the American

Library Association's Spectrum Scholarship Initiative, a program designed to recruit and award scholarships to individuals from underrepresented ethnic groups who want to obtain a graduate degree and leadership positions in the library field.

Currently, at the University of San Diego's Copley Library, Theresa meets with tenure-track librarians once a month, which can be time-consuming but is necessary. She also holds an annual retreat for her library team for professional development, rather than just strategic planning. When it comes to getting things done, she utilizes cross-functional committees in which either a librarian or a staff member can serve as a committee chair. As for overall advice, Theresa suggests making sure we develop people on an individual level and taking the time to find out what keeps people motivated. The time that leaders take to motivate and support their employees will pay off in creativity, innovation, project management, and organizational stability. My interview with Theresa follows.

What advice would you suggest for a new library director to diagnose any major internal problems so they can form a plan of action?

The first task that a new director must undertake is to introduce herself to the members of the library and to establish a rapport with the people in the organization. I recommend that the new director hold a meeting, especially for directors in small to medium libraries, to introduce herself to everyone and to briefly talk about her vision for the library. This step is important because the search committees for library directors or deans in academic institutions typically do not include many library personnel. The committees are typically composed of faculty and two to three library representatives. This means that many library employees were not involved in the search process to hire the director. All they know about the new director is based on what others have reported or on what they've read in the university's announcement about the new director.

Second, I suggest a new director take the time to personally meet with each employee if you are in an organization with seventy or fewer people. If you are in a larger organization, you may need to accomplish this step by holding a mix of either individual and department meetings, or you may opt to hold a town hall. I do not advise using technology for the purpose of introducing yourself to the organization because it is too impersonal. However, if you have a lot of satellite or international campuses, this might be an option until you can visit the site. The bottom line is that soon after the new director arrives on campus, it is essential for all library personnel to meet and hear from her. The value of face time for employees with a new leader is important because it humanizes you, and it is an indication of your interest in each person in the organization.

As a new director, it will be time-consuming to meet with employees. But do not take the easy way out by obtaining all of your information about the library from an associate director or associate university librarians. You want to hear directly from the librarians and staff. You can limit conversations to thirty minutes (though a few will exceed this limit). I also learned the hard way, so I urge you to establish rules for these conversations; for example, no employee should come into your office to talk about another staffer. Yes, library people will try to disparage the person they dislike the most in such meetings, if allowed. Make it clear that these conversations are for employees to tell you about their aspirations for the library, as well as for themselves. During these conversations, you can glean from people information not only about the library, but about their perspectives on the campus, local restaurants, and things to do in your new community.

Prepare yourself for at least one or two surprises about your new library. You will certainly discover some facts about the library that neither the search firm, the provost, nor the chair of the search committee shared with you during the interview process. For example, you may realize that not everyone in the library and on campus are one big happy family, or you may learn that between the time you accepted the job and started work, the university instituted a hiring freeze and cut budgets across campus by a percentage number. You may learn that you must implement a new library automation system or that you will be asked to eliminate employees. Occasionally, a new director arrives on campus and the provost who hired them is gone or leaves the university within a few months. All of these scenarios have happened to new directors. If you get a "surprise," take a deep breath and develop a plan of action to survive the challenge.

During your annual retreat, how do you determine the topics of interest? Do you have continual team-building workshops and exercises?

While holding a strategic planning retreat is popular in academic libraries, I have utilized retreats in three different organizations to get people to take a break from their daily work routine, to get people talking to each other, and as a professional development activity. At the University of San Diego's Copley Library, the five-member Retreat Committee is composed of both librarians and staff, as well as representatives from the three library departments. Key elements of the retreat are team-building exercises and hands-on group activities with a facilitator. To ensure that there are no distractions, the retreat is held at a local hotel. If you choose to hold a retreat at a hotel, the retreat space is often included for the price of buying lunch. Other locations for retreats include zoos, museums, hiking trails, parks, and outdoor adventure activities, or any location or activity that your library team thinks is appropriate. You may even have a facility on campus that can be used for your retreat, but it should be located some distance from the library to prevent people from going to their offices at lunchtime and throughout the day. The staff sharing the noon meal together is an important aspect of the retreat experience.

On retreat day, employees are asked to avoid sitting next to someone in their department or with a personal friend. The idea is to get people in the organization to spend the day talking with individuals they do not know well. Copley's Retreat Committee effectively assigns all attendees to a table with this fact in mind. I recommend hiring a facilitator for the day, or two facilitators if you have different topics for the morning and afternoon programs. Having a facilitator enables the director to be a part of the team on retreat day. It is imperative that the director clear her calendar for the day, arrive on time, and be fully engaged in the retreat. She should not pop in and out of the room dealing with other business or sit at the back of the room doing e-mail. Everyone will take their cue from the director in terms of whether the retreat is important. Moreover, it is a good idea to pick your retreat location early and to establish when this annual conclave takes place. In one previous library I worked in, the annual retreat was held during the summer. In the Copley Library, it is held in January because the university has a long intercession. For your retreat day, establish a few ground rules, such as no cell phones, attendees should arrive on time and stay for the entire day, attendees agree to be active participants, they agree to respect others' opinions, and so on.

How does your organization resolve conflict and disagreement while still maintaining a positive outlook?

The answer to dealing with organizational conflict is managing culture and people. The culture of a library will determine the amount of conflict that will exist in an organization. If the culture is negative or there is a hostile work environment, the library is going to be a contentious and highly stressful place to work. While it is difficult to change culture, it can be done, but it will take time. Hiring highly skilled librarians and staff who are a good fit in their positions can go a long way toward reducing personnel conflicts. To eliminate conflict and a negative culture, a new director must hire the right people. In his book *Good to Great,* Jim Collins advises that "getting the right people on the bus, the wrong people off the bus, and the right people in the right seats" is needed to create change (Collins 2011). He goes on to say, "Great vision without great people is irrelevant." I concur. The most problematic people in a library are people who are disappointed with their position. These employees tend to underperform and to create chaos in the organization. If there is no room for advancement or position rightsizing for them in the library, you can work with such individuals to leave the organization. Very often, though, employees who fall into this category are not motivated to leave the library and obtain the position that they want. In these cases, proceed with building your organization, as you will never have everyone on board. Once you hire good people, treat them well. Ensure that they have a clear position description, and establish annual goals for all employees in your organization. Incentivize employees to be good workers through merit raises, professional development and travel, and other forms of acknowledgment.

Holding a variety of meetings is important to maintaining a healthy organization. I work with a three-person Management Team that meets monthly to discuss topics. These meetings assist in mitigating problems. I also meet monthly with each tenure-track librarian and any librarians who are working on projects. These meetings allow an exchange of information between the librarian and me, and it provides the librarian with a chance to apprise me of their work and to talk with me about any concerns. Librarians are required to come to these meetings with a written agenda. Likewise, I informally interact with staff as I move throughout the building or see them on campus. This provides staff with an opportunity to ask me a question about something they are inquisitive about or have heard a rumor about in the library. The library faculty meetings, which are held twice a month, have a formal agenda, minutes, and deliberations with voting. Additionally, several library-wide department meetings are held throughout the year.

What types of "soft leadership skills" are you looking for in your leadership team, committee team leaders, and project managers?

The first soft skill that I look for in an employee, especially a leader/manager, is emotional intelligence. Daniel Goleman states: "Emotional intelligence [EI] refers to the capacity for recognizing our own feelings and those of others, for motivating ourselves, and for managing emotions well in ourselves and in our relationships. It describes abilities distinct from, but complementary to, academic intelligence, the purely cognitive capacities measured by IQ" (Goleman 2005). EI, not intellect, makes the difference in whether a person succeeds in a library, if we consider that everyone holds an ALA-accredited master's degree.

In addition, it is not a bad idea for a library to have at least one optimist, one empathetic person, and one risk-taker to balance the management team, committees, or the overall organization.

How do you balance between your traditional administrative, fundraising, and leadership responsibilities while also creating an internal environment where all employees are engaged and productive?

A leader must be passionate, committed, and a hard worker, and she must view the juggling of administrative work, fundraising, and managing the library environment as part of the strategy she uses to achieve her vision for the library. Such an approach will keep the director focused and motivated. The director must have significant education and experience, as well as a deep expertise in all facets of librarianship. This knowledge will enable her to easily multitask and switch tasks throughout the day. There is no time for significant on-the-job training in a leadership position. Undoubtedly, the work ethic must be such that the director is willing to rise early and stay late at work to accomplish goals or to meet deadlines. I recommend that a leader hire an effective wizard-like administrative assistant who is an excellent multitasker and who can support and keep the leader on track as she tackles competing obligations each day. The director must delegate to her managers and trust them to take care of their areas so she can focus on both internal and external obligations. ■ ■ ■

REFERENCES

Beck, Randall J., and Jim Harter. 2019. "Why Great Managers Are So Rare." Gallup. www.gallup.com/workplace/231593/why-great-managers-rare.

Chamorro-Premuzic, Tomas. 2017. "To Prevent Burnout, Hire Better Bosses." *Harvard Business Review* 8, no. 3: 4.

Collins, Jim. 2011. *Good to Great: Why Some Companies Make the Leap . . . and Others Don't*. HarperCollins.

Crowley, Mark C. 2015. "How the Wrong People Get Promoted and How to Change It." April 29. Fast Company. www.fastcompany.com/3045453/how-the-wrong -people-get-promoted-and-how-to-change-it.

Daniels, Aubrey. 2016. *Bringing Out the Best in People: How to Apply the Astonishing Power of Positive Reinforcement*. 3rd edition. McGraw-Hill Education.

Goleman, Daniel. 2005. *Emotional Intelligence*. Bantam.

Runyon, W. 2017. "Practical Thinking about Employment Engagement." *Workforce Solutions Review* 8, no. 2: 5.

Trust

After leadership and management, developing, repairing, and strengthening trust in the organization is always the second most important factor in attaining a healthy work environment and high employee engagement. The gold standard for research on workplace culture is the global analytics firm called Great Place to Work (www.greatplacetowork.com). Great Place to Work has been around for thirty years and is known for its Trust Index Survey, which is taken annually by millions of employees from thousands of organizations, and its Trust Model, which has guided research on workplace culture for decades. During my phone conversations and interactions with the Great Place to Work staff, they had an amazingly simple explanation for why trust is so important. Lack of trust affects employees' need for safety and security, which is one of the basic needs within an organization. When an existing lack of trust is not addressed for a long period of time, the workplace culture moves toward more incivility, hostility, and lower morale. The common saying in a distrustful environment is: "Why bother to make an effort when the organization clearly does not care about me?"

Great Place to Work created the Trust Model, which has five dimensions:

1. Credibility—Leadership and management are believable and trust-worthy.
2. Respect—Employees are respected for their talents regardless of where they are in the organization.
3. Fairness—Employees need to believe that management's practices and policies are fair, impartial, and equitable.
4. Pride—Employees need to feel that their individual impact is making a difference within the organization. No one wants to feel like they are disposable or easily replaced.
5. Camaraderie—Employees want the organization to be a place where their colleagues and management are supportive, friendly, and welcoming. (Great Place to Work 2018)

If an organization has a lack of trust, these dimensions can serve as a guidepost for getting the organization back on track or identifying what might be going wrong. However, keep in mind that this is not an overnight fix; building or restoring trust takes time, and most new managers say it takes six months to a year of consistent messaging and actions to regain the staff's trust once it has been lost.

WHEN TRUST GOES WRONG, NOTHING GOES RIGHT

The following is one example where toxic leadership has eroded trust within an organization.

One employee I interviewed, James, works as a librarian at a small liberal arts college. James explained that from the outside, the academic library looks like a dream job; the college has a high profile, is well-funded, and has an excellent research reputation. Inside the organization, however, there is constant infighting among colleagues, bullying, turf wars, and suspicion. The college is also on its third library director in ten years, and she just received her termination notice and will be leaving next year. When I inquired about this high turnover in the library administration, James corrected me and said that the library directors are pushed out, but the senior library administrators remain the same and are the real people running the library. It is the senior administrators who set the tone in the organization, and this has resulted in intimidation, silent treatments, passive-aggressive power plays, and disheartening annual reviews. Over the several years that James has worked in the library, the selection committee (which is usually the senior administration and outside volunteers) tends to pick a library director with a similar disposition (bullying, divisive) to run the organization. Because the library's employees can vote the library director out through a vote of no confidence, they can get rid of the person at the top, but the real culprits remain in their posts at the organization. My next question was, why didn't someone go above the library administration to voice their concerns? Hadn't the college administration noticed a problem with the constant turnover of library directors? James said that one person did raise the alarm and took it to the college administration, but that person was marginalized, harassed, alienated, and eventually resigned. At the time, the college administration sided with the library's leadership, so everyone else got scared and kept their head down. However, with this last firing, the campus administration finally listened to reason and the senior administrators were finally told to step down and take library faculty positions.

In this example, the good news is that the organization will hire a new leadership team. The bad news is that the new leadership team (if the campus recruits wisely) will still have to spend considerable time rebuilding trust after years of low engagement and low morale. This will be compounded due to the fact that the old regime is still employed in the library—though no longer in positions of power. But raising the library staff's morale may have a chance if the campus administration and the selection committee members recruit new leaders who display the soft skills mentioned in chapter 1. However, if they bring in new leaders who do not have the skills, patience, and aptitude to turn the organization around, the library could be in for a major setback.

WHAT DOES "TRUST" LOOK LIKE IN AN ORGANIZATION?

Trust is simple to understand but can be hard to maintain. For many, trust is simply a feeling of confidence in others. Trust is elicited by a person's sincerity, reliability, and competence. Employees want to feel that they can trust what leaders, managers, and supervisors say, and that they follow through with their promises and are competent to lead the organization. Another important ingredient of trust is that leaders should have the employees' best interests at heart. This is crucial especially during times of strife or when delivering bad news such as budget cuts, layoffs, or a major organizational restructuring. Employees need to know that their leaders are fighting for them and care about their overall well-being. Overall, the leadership must create a positive environment where people feel that their individual talents, skills, and abilities can shine regardless of their position in the organization.

HOW TO CREATE AND MANAGE TRUST

Creating and sustaining a positive trust culture starts with the leadership, but almost everyone in the organization must be involved for long-term change to be successful. For leaders who have inherited a distrustful, toxic, or low morale environment, patience is the key for both them and the employees. On average, you should expect a positive change in trust culture to take anywhere from 6–8 months to 2 years to occur, depending on how long the dysfunctional culture was tolerated without intervention.

If you are a new manager, supervisor, or leader, here are some well-documented strategies for creating cultures of trust; these will raise oxytocin levels, create greater empathy among employees, and improve organizational behavior and trust:

1. *Recognize excellence*—I will talk more about this topic in chapter 3, but sincere recognition and praise for your employees' unique talents and skills is one of the fastest ways to increase engagement and build goodwill. In most organizations, people rarely hear praise or receive positive reinforcement for their individual work unless they have gone above and beyond the call of duty. But many times, you can make someone's day by showing that you "see" them during the course of the day or week. Never be stingy with praise and actively find ways to build positive self-esteem in the workplace.
2. *Empower employees to choose their work patterns and habits*—Giving employees some autonomy and control over their working conditions communicates that leadership and direct supervisors trust them. Trust requires that the leadership provide employees with the tools, resources, and support they need, and then take their hands off the

wheel. This is not a "one size fits all" approach, but a conversation within each department about what working conditions will stimulate greater employee engagement can be very helpful. From there, the organization can have a pilot project to see how these changes impact productivity and morale. That way, the organization can try new things without feeling that those changes will immediately be permanent.

3. *Give employees a voice in their own job design*—Employees should be allowed to give input on the projects they work on and how they will approach the assignment. This should allow them to select projects that align with their unique skill sets and abilities, which will result in more engagement and ultimately a better product or service.

4. *Communicate often*—Frequent "check-ins," along with both formal and informal interactions, will keep an open dialogue going, which helps build trust. These interactions are better when they are informal and consistent, which gets people into a more natural rhythm to talk openly. At my current remote job, our team talks on the phone every Monday morning to discuss our week and chat about life and potential obstacles. This consistent schedule works wonders for building rapport and trust as a small remote team that spends a great deal of time working alone.

5. *Intentionally build relationships*—When leadership creates a work environment where people form friendships and have fun, employees are 43 percent more likely to report having received recognition at work. Take time to bring people together for happy hours, birthday and holiday celebrations, work celebrations for accomplishing mini-goals, and larger celebrations for major milestones. Interactions which make people feel like they are part of a winning team that is accomplishing overall good work can go a long way to building and strengthening trust.

6. *Show vulnerability*—People want their leaders to be competent, but they also appreciate it when leaders ask for input and advice, and admit that they do not have all the answers; this tends to strengthen trust. Paul Zak's research shows that the most emotionally connected leaders let employees know that they need their help to build and grow the organization (Zak 2017).

TRUST: OVERALL RECOMMENDATIONS

- If there is a lack of trust in the organization, check to see if there is a gap in one of the five trust dimensions: credibility, respect, fairness, pride, and camaraderie.
- If there is a lack of trust in the organization, do not assume that it will automatically get better; it takes time and hard work for things to turn around. Make sure that the organization is dedicating time and attention on improving and strengthening trust. Paying attention to levels of trust in an organization before it becomes dysfunctional will not only add to more efficiency down the line, but will also spare long-term hurt feelings that can affect employee engagement.
- Always level with the staff. Even if the news is bad, make sure that the leadership maintains a level of credibility and commitment to support the people who are helping run the organization.
- Communicate frequently. Make sure that the messages are frequent and consistent and are disseminated through different mediums. The larger the organization, the more communication avenues that are needed.
- In order to get trust, you must give trust. Managers tell me all the time that employees are lazy, up to no good, and must be watched in order to make sure they are doing their job. However, people can sense when you do not trust them, and in turn they will not trust management or the organization. One person summed it up this way: trust that people will rise to the occasion, give them the right tools and resources to get the job done, and then get out of their way.
- And lastly, review your organization's policies and management styles to make sure that negative reinforcement, penalty, and punishment are not being used excessively. Positive reinforcement will often be more effective.

SUCCESS STORIES

The following three success stories are from new library directors who took over organizations that were suffering from a lack of trust. Each of these leaders has their own style and approach, but they all agreed that rebuilding trust was the first item on their agenda for creating positive change in the organization.

INTERVIEW WITH
Nancy S. Kirkpatrick, Consortium Director

Nancy S. Kirkpatrick is the executive director and CEO of the OhioNET library consortium. Prior to moving to Ohio, she served as associate director of the Midwest Collaborative for Library Services from 2015 to 2018 and as director of library services at Marian University in Indianapolis from 2011 to 2015.

A former attorney, Nancy has enjoyed facilitating and mediating conversations for individuals and organizations for as long as she can remember. She was introduced to appreciative inquiry (AI) principles in 2018 and has incorporated them into her organizational leadership style, her facilitation services, and her personal life.

Nancy has a bachelor's degree in journalism, a law degree from the T. C. Williams School of Law at the University of Richmond, and an MLIS degree from the University of Illinois at Urbana-Champaign.

When Nancy first arrived at OhioNET, she wanted to give her team a voice to express ideas that inspire creativity and innovation. She accomplished this by establishing an open-door policy and holding individual one-on-ones with every member of the OhioNET team. The purpose of these sessions was twofold: to hear the concerns or issues that had arisen in the past and to ask about each individual's aspirations for the future of the organization. After spending some time on the job, Nancy noticed that the organization was very traditionally hierarchical and siloed, despite its small size. In response, she has encouraged teamwork and collaboration by reviving weekly team meetings. During these meetings, Nancy encourages her staff to celebrate by using a 3-and-1 approach—they share their top three accomplishments of the week and bring up one problem where they may be stuck and need group input. By focusing on achievements and then encouraging problem-solving, Nancy has inspired the staff to try new things in a safe space. Another major game changer was allowing all the staff to work remotely at least one day a week. This flexibility went a long way to increasing trust, and it mirrored today's workplace engagement trends. Nancy stressed to me that she is just getting started with her work, and she will continue coaching, training, and creating opportunities for her staff to excel as professionals.

As a new consortium director, what recommendations would you give for someone to start a positive workplace culture campaign?

I would encourage them to explore the history of their organization. Spending a little time getting to know and understand what created the current workplace culture (both positive and challenging) may provide context down the road when it comes to situations and personalities. I recommend reading broadly about positive workplace culture, and specifically with an eye toward organizations outside of libraries. It is easy to talk to our colleagues and see what works (or does not) for them, but we can also learn from our peers in other fields. We should open ourselves to reliable information from a variety of sources and review those sources regularly.

Once you have a plan of action, test some ideas to see what types of things speak to your team and identify who on your team is ready for change. Building positive momentum will require having some internal champions on your side. Be open and transparent in your communication and in your plans.

How does your organization handle conflict? How did you work with staff members who may be resistant to change?

Choosing the best way to handle conflict is dependent on the context. There are times when involving HR is not only prudent but perhaps required, but that is another article. I try to get an understanding of what the conflict is and what the cause is—misinformation, misunderstanding, whatever. Once I have a sense of the what, we can tackle the why and the what next. Conflict resolution involves listening, acknowledging the perspective of others, and then finding a solution. My solutions do not always make everyone happy, but they are fair and equitable, and they keep the needs of our entire organization at their core.

Change can be scary, even when you know it is necessary. And though I came in knowing some things that I wanted to change immediately (or at least I thought I did), I took time to assess the landscape before instituting any changes. I needed the team to get comfortable with me before I asked them to try things outside their comfort zone. I asked questions about what worked and what did not and what might look different if things were how we wanted them to be. We identified a shared vision and then brainstormed about what we needed to do to get there. Some changes were small and easy, while some were huge with a much larger impact. No matter the change, clear and consistent communication was key. Also, if I did not know something, I said so. There is no shame in not having all the answers.

Do you have any specific guidelines for remote work? Do you have your staff accomplish specific tasks when they are at home?

I do not have any specific guidelines for remote work, but I do have some recommendations. Identify a communication channel that works for your staff (we use Microsoft Teams in addition to phone and e-mail) and can keep people connected no matter where they are physically working. Use this channel regularly so it becomes second nature. People need to know they can reach their teammates and get a timely response. Good communication builds trust.

I do not micromanage my staff, so they (or their managers) determine what projects work better from a remote location versus our main office. Personally, I have set up my schedule so that when I'm working remotely, I focus on projects that require uninterrupted time to delve deeply. My time in the office is focused on more collaborative projects. The bottom line is that you must hire the right people and trust them to manage their time.

In the course of encouraging teamwork, collaboration, and innovation, have you seen any changes that would positively impact your customers?

I believe that all the positive changes we are making to our internal work environment have a direct and positive impact on our customers—that is, our member libraries. The changes we are implementing are making our workflows more efficient and more user-friendly. This enables us to answer inquiries faster and provide a better online experience. All of this work requires collaboration and a willingness to try new things. It is also important to recognize that everything we try will not succeed, and that is okay. Encouraging innovation means accepting failures and learning from those as well.

What are you looking for in terms of soft skills for new employees? How do you balance technical expertise with soft skills?

We are currently in a growth phase at OhioNET, having just filled three new positions that will start in January, so this question is quite timely. In all our positions, I try to strike a balance between technical expertise and soft skills. The soft skills I look for include emotional intelligence and self-awareness, the ability to work on a team and be respectful of one's colleagues, and the willingness to ask for help or guidance when needed. Additionally, adaptability and some creative problem-solving skills are always welcome. I don't have a specific ratio in mind for balancing technical versus soft skills; rather, I think it's important to look at the skill set of the entire team and try to make sure that we're balanced as a whole.

What is your vision for your organization in terms of employee engagement and workplace morale in the next two years?

As I just mentioned, we are growing our team, which provides a wonderful opportunity to engage with everyone on the staff and seek their input as we move forward. One way I do this is to ask open-ended questions using a channel on Microsoft Teams. These questions generally follow appreciative inquiry principles and can be as simple as "What makes you feel positive at work?" Or the questions may require a bit more thought, such as "In the (Ohio) library landscape, where do you hear opportunity knocking? And how can we answer it?"

For those who want to perhaps remain anonymous, I have also tried another approach. There is a draft of our strategic plan on the walls in our office, along with sticky notes and markers. I have put it up for a month, asking everyone to spend some time reflecting and brainstorming individually or in groups—whatever works for them—and then adding their comments to the plan. After the month is up, we will take a look as a team and see how we want to change or adapt our plan based on what motivates us.

I ask these questions to learn what is important to the team, what drives them, and where I should look for opportunities moving forward. I believe if we are engaged in work that matters to us individually, it will motivate us on those days when we question whether our work really matters. ■ ■ ■

INTERVIEW WITH
Consuella Askew, Library Director

Consuella Askew is the director of the John Cotton Dana Library, on the Rutgers-Newark campus of Rutgers University. She formerly served as the associate dean for public services at Florida International University. Prior to that, Consuella held chief librarian positions in two of the CUNY system's libraries. She also worked at the Association of Research Libraries for three years in the Statistics and Measurement Program, and she has held professional positions at the libraries of Howard University and Broward Community College.

When Consuella became the director at the John Cotton Dana Library, she quickly noticed that employee morale was low and there were tough decisions that needed to be made due to looming budget cuts. So she did her due diligence by talking with the staff, community members, faculty, and other stakeholders before making any changes. One of the hardest decisions she made was changing the library's leadership and reporting structure. As one might expect, being reclassified was hard because some staff members enjoyed the title of "supervisor" even if it did not come with any extra salary. To make sure she kept everyone informed during the reorganization, Consuella continued to have frequent meetings to explain how the changes benefit the organization long term and how the new structure was more in alignment with the library's goals.

When you first discovered that you needed to make some hard changes in your organization, what were your first steps as a new library director?

When I first arrived at the John Cotton Dana Library, there were several things that needed my immediate attention. First, the library is in a unique position because it is part of the Rutgers University Library System, but it is also an integral part of the Rutgers-Newark campus. The chancellor of the Rutgers-Newark campus informed me she loved the library, but there needed to be some changes to meet the future needs of the faculty, scholars, and students. In addition, the staff had some trust and low morale issues that resulted from the previous library administration that needed to be addressed. So, I approached this new challenge by listening to every staff member and staying true to my word not to commit to making immediate changes. By introducing the idea but not making any sudden moves, I allowed people to get used to new ideas and suggestions without the fear of retaliation.

How often did you need to interact with your staff during the reorganization? What did you do when there was resistance to the new ideas?

Well, I decided to let the staff take the lead in the new strategic plan. The Rutgers library formed a strategic plan committee to look at current and future trends and eventually work with an internal consultant who facilitated a larger planning session with everyone. I did meet with the committee to get updates and provide them with important information from my interactions with the campus administration. But trusting that the committee would get the work done created a more collaborative environment where the staff felt more in control of determining their future directions. This did not stop people from being scared of change, but they at least felt they were part of the process. I also let everyone know that some of the changes we were making were critical for our future because of potential budget cuts. I wanted them to know that I wanted to fight to keep everyone employed, so becoming more efficient now would keep us ahead of the curve in the future.

How did you keep the staff engaged and optimistic for the future? How was this reinforced with your leadership team?

I encouraged the leadership team to spend quality time in every department to answer all questions and concerns that resulted from the new strategic plan. I also spent time sitting down with people and answering their questions about the plan and our flexibility in implementing it. In all honesty, there were a few people who do not like the new strategic plan or the changes, but that is a natural occurrence. As a leader you stay honest and steady and stay flexible in the implementation because there are bound to be changes with new information. I went in knowing it was going to take time, and this was more of a long-term plan than one of immediate gratification.

How did you build a culture of trust once you found out that the staff were still terrified from the previous administration?

Building trust takes time. It is important to be honest, listen to the staff, and be a steady force that is fighting for both staff and crucial resources for the library. The new leader must be reliable, true to their word, and in many cases get out of the way and allow staff to do their work. Stepping back from the new strategic plan was big because it allowed the staff to work as a team and set future directions. ■ ■ ■

Alexia Hudson-Ward: How to Build Trust

Alexia Hudson-Ward is currently an associate for research and learning at the MIT Libraries. I discussed trust with her when she was in her previous position, the Azariah Smith Root Director of Libraries for Oberlin College and Conservatory. In less than three years she had reenvisioned one of the nation's oldest liberal arts college library systems into an agile and creative organization through role recasting and the strategic positioning of public and technical services as central to the pedagogical mission of the institution. This shift has resulted in the Oberlin College Libraries being ranked as the institution's top administrative unit and achieving high marks for trans-unit collaboration on campus in recent surveys.

I met Alexia years ago when we were new academic librarians. Alexia came from a corporate background, which I could tell right away from her no-nonsense, "here are the facts" way of approaching problems. When a friend referred me to Alexia for her leadership work, I knew that something positive was going to result. Though I had approached Alexia for the leadership chapter, our conversation led to a discussion about trust and DEI work.

Trust

When Alexia started as the library director at Oberlin, she saw that there were noticeable challenges between staff that were causing stagnation in advancing new and innovative practices. Alexia took action by conducting informal internal surveys and open-door sessions. From there, she prioritized concerns and empowered her staff to make decisions. By giving them some freedom to make their own choices, she was able to impart a strong sense of accomplishment. There was also a celebration of small wins and an acknowledgment that the organization was moving forward in a positive direction. As the organization continued to rack up smaller wins, Alexia was able to build confidence among the staff that she would follow through with her promises and was committed to success. Alexia is currently looking at the performance evaluation process for non-unionized staff to make sure that the process is as equitable as possible.

Trust and the Correlation with Diversity Initiatives

Alexia's success in making significant strides in diversity, equity, and inclusion resulted from creating a space to have difficult conversations and not expecting the culture to change overnight. She began by building a foundation of trust and respect for all employees in order to make behavioral changes in this critical area. She was already developing several task forces, and Alexia decided to chair the diversity committee herself to get things off the ground. By leading the DEI task force that first year, Alexia was able to set the tempo by problem-solving (celebrating small wins) and allowing people room to talk things through in an open and supportive environment. Her overall advice for achieving success in DEI is to create an environment of mutual trust and respect in which the staff feel free to talk through prejudices, stereotypes, and misconceptions. Today, they are working through their job descriptions and their recruiting practices to create a framework that will attract top talent to the organization.

REFERENCES

Great Place to Work. 2018. "Trust Model: The Definition of a Great Workplace." www.greatplacetowork.com/trust-model.

Peters, Kim. 2018. "5 Facts about Great Place to Work Certification." September 17. McKnight's Long-Term Care News. www.mcknights.com/blogs/guest-columns/5-facts-about-great-place-to-work-certification/.

Zak, Paul J. 2017. "The Neuroscience of Trust." *Harvard Business Review*, January/February: 4.

Recognition and Praise

f leadership and trust are the foundations for employee engagement, recognition and praise are the secret weapons that can benefit every organization. Employee recognition and praise are continuously cited as an effective management strategy to sustain a positive work environment. However, recognition and praise are commonly underutilized and are usually not brought out until the annual review or the yearly staff appreciation award celebration. Annual reviews and award celebrations are a great start, but they only scratch the surface of what can be done to improve staff morale, a sense of belonging, and individual recognition.

WHAT IS EMPLOYEE RECOGNITION?

Employee recognition and praise are specific and targeted strategies to recognize individual employees' contributions to the organization. Employee praise focuses on what people are doing right (positive reinforcement) instead of ignoring the person's contributions or only responding when someone has done something wrong (negative reinforcement, penalty, and punishment). Most people in organizations say that they are usually ignored at work or very occasionally get a cursory "great job" for their efforts.

The Invisible Worker: The Benefits of Being "Recognized"

During a hotel stay, the housekeeper wanted to get a head start with my room, so I let her in while I was gathering my items for the day. Instead of my normally rushing out the door, what started out as a casual conversation with her changed my worldview about recognition and praise. The housekeeper's name was Stephanie, and she informed me that she was in the process of getting a special education teacher's certification. Her housekeeping job allowed her to pay the bills and complete her education, but she hated being "the invisible person" at work. Hotel housekeeping is a grueling, thankless job where most guests barely acknowledge your existence. In the four years she had worked at the hotel, Stephanie could count on the fingers of one hand the number of guests who had taken any interest in her as a person. When I mentioned the traditional money left on the nightstand, Stephanie agreed that it is a nice gesture but is also an easy way to stay disconnected. Stephanie chose special education as a major because she wanted to dedicate her life to changing the lives of people who are deemed "invisible." We chatted for a few minutes longer before I had to leave for my meeting. When I returned to the room at the end of the day, Stephanie had left some extra items in my room (a complimentary bottle of water, additional toiletries, and the hotel's chocolate chip cookies). The chocolate chip cookies were there because I had raved about how delicious they were, but I needed to stay away from them. We had both laughed about Stephanie's own love for chocolate chip cookies, but her thighs told her to stop the madness. I told her that my thighs stay mad at me because of my addiction to French fries and potato chips. That night, I wrote a quick letter on the hotel memo pad and dropped it off to her boss thanking Stephanie for the lovely room, the cookies, and the warm hospitality, and conveying my best wishes that she become a special education teacher. Well, twenty-four hours later, upon returning to my room after a long day, the hotel manager sent me up complimentary French fries and a cocktail for being such a lovely guest. I teased Stephanie before I checked out and told her that my thighs were not happy, but of course I'd enjoyed the French fries and the glass of wine.

After returning home from the conference, I reflected on the housekeeper's accuracy on how easy it is to become an invisible person. A little recognition and praise for a good job had instantly brought out the best in everyone. Stephanie and the management team made sure I had a wonderful experience and went above and beyond my expectations. In turn I was excited to write an overwhelmingly positive "Tripadvisor" review about the hotel, the management, and the excellent housekeeping staff. When I was relaying my experiences to my work colleagues who were also staying at the hotel, they were shocked that I received so many "extras" while their hotel experience was average or mediocre at best. I am ashamed to admit that normally I would have been right there with them pointing out the hotel's flaws, small mishaps, and minor mistakes as we commiserated on what was wrong instead of what was right. But this time it was not the flaws, mishaps, and mistakes that I focused on (they were still there), but the positive experience I'd had.

After that lovely encounter, whenever I spend time at the hotel, I always write a personal thank-you note to the housekeeper with specific comments that I observed from the room, and I wish the housekeeper a relaxing day outside of work. What is interesting is that this feeling of gratitude usually extends beyond housekeeping and I find myself consistently thanking the doorman, the front desk staff, the maintenance people, and anyone else I come into contact with at the hotel. As a result, I have received a better hotel experience in terms of complimentary upgrades, extra toiletries, additional reward points, and late checkouts. But another unforeseen benefit is that I have become a better hotel guest, and in this state of gratitude, the outcomes continue to exceed my expectations.

MASLOW'S HIERARCHY OF NEEDS

Abraham Maslow's famous "hierarchy of needs" is a five-tier model of human needs in the form of a pyramid, with basic physiological needs (food, water, warmth, etc.) at the bottom and self-actualization (achieving one's full potential as a human being) at the top. The theory says that a human being cannot get to the highest level (self-actualization) until they have successfully moved upward through the lower levels or categories. Although Maslow's hierarchy is commonly used in psychology, it is also a great theory to help us understand the different emotional levels that people experience in the workplace.

In Maslow's hierarchy of needs, there are five distinct levels or tiers: from the bottom up, they are the basic physiological ones (food, shelter, clothing, warmth); safety and security; love, intimacy, and belonging; esteem (prestige and a sense of self-accomplishment); and the highest level, self-actualization. According to the article "Maslow's Hierarchy of Needs Explained," in Maslow's theory, as a lower need is successfully met, the person's focus naturally turns to satisfying the next higher need in the pyramid (Hopper 2019).

The first need, *physiological,* is the person's basic physical need for food, clothing, and shelter. When it comes to the workplace, this translates into money. If a job pays employees enough that they can pay their rent and utilities and buy food and clothing, then the job satisfies their basic physical needs.

The second need is *safety,* which we strive for both at home and at work. Employees must have safety and security if they are to succeed in the workplace. Employees need to feel that their jobs are secure, and they do not want to constantly worry about being laid off or fired. If the leadership's motivational strategy is to threaten employees with the loss of their jobs to improve their job performance, this may work as a short-term strategy, but it will backfire over the long term because it undermines the basic human need for safety.

The third need is *love and belonging,* which is our need to feel loved, accepted, and connected with others in our personal, social, and work relationships. Employees work better if they have an easy rapport with their boss and coworkers. If employees feel alienated from the company, their work performance will suffer or in many cases remain stagnant.

The fourth need is *esteem,* or feeling good about ourselves. At work, this need boils down to having our individual contributions and achievements seen as valuable and important. Self-esteem is how much the employee likes and values himself. The best organizations create both formal and informal programs to build up work self-esteem and create an environment where all people thrive and excel.

The fifth and highest need in the pyramid is *self-actualization,* that is, living up to our full potential as human beings. Satisfying this need may involve feeling that our work and contributions are making an impact, and we are living up to our full potential in life and are using our creativity and passion. This is where the employees have become better versions of themselves at work, and in terms of the organization, this is where the workplace is attaining maximum levels of productivity, efficiency, creative energy, and innovation.

Getting a paycheck with the traditional benefits is usually seen as a sufficient motivation for all employees. I hear all the time that the employees are getting paid well or they receive excellent benefits so that should be enough to produce consistent high performance. However, when we look at Maslow's pyramid, getting a paycheck with excellent benefits only fulfills the first and second needs (*physiological* and *safety*) along the continuum. Most organizations want their employees to strive for excellence, creativity, innovation, and productivity (*self-actualization*), but this cannot be accomplished unless there is an inclusive environment (*belonging*) and employees' contributions are recognized as valuable (*esteem*). In other words, an organization cannot achieve its highest level of functioning (through employees' *self-actualization*) until the employees' four more basic needs have been met first. An important corollary of this is that developing a strategy to increase organizational belonging and esteem is also the foundation for attaining greater diversity, equity, and inclusion.

REASONS FOR LACK OF RECOGNITION AND PRAISE

Recognition and praise fit nicely into creating more belonging (inclusive) environments and inculcating esteem (feelings of accomplishment) in employees, so why is this fruitful strategy not used more in organizations? To find the answer, I talked to managers and directors nationwide to see if there was any potential resistance to providing more recognition and praise at work. When I asked if they knew definitively if the direct supervisors were offering recognition and praise, usually the answer was "no" or a referral to talk to the supervisors. Direct supervisors or in some cases middle managers were more resistant to using continuous individualized recognition and praise as a strategy. The following are some of the top reasons that were given to not provide too much recognition and praise:

1. *It is wrong to thank someone for doing their job*—Employees are hired to do a job and they receive both compensation and benefits for their work. If they are not doing their work, other people will be more than willing to take their place. The only time you need to acknowledge a person is if they go above and beyond or excel beyond your expectations.

2. *Constant recognition will lead to feelings of entitlement*—Supervisors warned me that if they constantly recognized and praised the employees, they would become complacent or arrogant and expect positive reinforcement even if it is not warranted.
3. *Managers have too many direct reports*—Managers spoke about feeling overworked and overwhelmed, and the obligation to bestow recognition and praise just added one more thing to their growing list of responsibilities. They feel that the annual review is the perfect time to thank people for doing a good job.
4. *We thank people once a year during the annual Staff Appreciation Day*—That should be enough!

When we ignore our employees except once a year, or expect constant self-motivation to keep people engaged, we are doing the organization a disservice in terms of innovation, growth, and creative thinking. I always find that when you go into an organization and the consensus is that the company is stuck in a rut, resistant to change, or full of people not putting in much effort at work, you always find a lack of recognition and praise as one of the major factors. Using multiple strategies to boost employees' self-esteem is essential to elevate the morale of the organization and encourage employee engagement.

SEVEN IDEAS FOR EMPLOYEE RECOGNITION AND PRAISE

So, what are some ideas to incorporate into your recognition and praise toolkit? The following ideas are not a comprehensive list but are proven techniques to help an organization get started. My suggestion is that you explore these suggestions (and others) and then pick and choose whichever ones work best for your specific organization.

Peer-to-peer recognition—A peer recognition program, whether formal or informal, should be a part of an organization's recognition strategy. In this program, employees acknowledge their fellow employees' talents and accomplishments. There is a great deal of research on peer-to-peer programs that utilize everything from Post-it notes to kudo message boards, to reward bucks, to departmental celebrations and formal programs with advanced software. The key is to start small, make sure that everyone gets a chance to be included, and build from there.

Handwritten notes—For conveying praise and recognition, typed notes or text messages are nice, but handwritten notes, thank-you cards, and letters take it to the next level. When I was a director, I would keep handwritten notes from my employees thanking me for being a great boss. I would reread these great cards and letters when I was having a bad day or implementing a policy that I did not agree with and needed to refocus my messaging to stand up for and support my employees. In turn I noticed that my employees also kept my handwritten notes thanking them for their individual contributions to a project on their desks or placed on their walls. Some staff would repeat verbatim what I wrote to them several years past because they enjoyed the personal and individualized feedback. The extra effort is usually appreciated by everyone.

Employee wall of fame—An "employee wall of fame" is a vehicle for visual reminders of success stories. The wall should recognize individual accomplishments, along with departmental contributions. This should not be a competition but a way for everyone to see themselves in a positive light.

Just-in-time recognition—When you see something done well, say something. Just-in-time compliments are the best. If you know someone is working on an assignment or project that has a deadline, once the deadline is met, praise them for a job well done. This just-in-time feedback will not only feel good to the employee, but also will provide positive reinforcement for their doing just as well on future assignments.

Newsletters' praise—Let your external customers know that your staff are rock stars in your library's newsletter. Do not highlight just one person, but multiple people in the publication, and make sure you rotate the praise so that it is not just the high achievers who are recognized. This not only makes the staff feel appreciated, but your customers will notice the positive energy in your library.

Thank-you meeting—Call people to a meeting (without telling them why) and then thank them one by one for their individual accomplishments on a not-so-specific occasion. Do this just because it's Tuesday, and the meeting will be great for an organizational pick-me-up.

Sponsor a volunteer day—Individual staff members can take company time to volunteer for their favorite charity, or the whole library staff can decide together on a cause and then volunteer for it together. Not only does this benefit and give back to the community, but in many cases, people come back to work recharged and energized. Working together also strengthens the bonds of the organization as a "work family" (belonging, inclusiveness) and provides staffers with opportunities to see people outside of their normal jobs.

NEVER SATISFIED AS A MOTIVATOR

The following is a true story of a new library director who was trying to motivate his staff to strive for excellence by telling them a personal tale about his motivation and drive at work. The library director's heart was in the right place, but his message drew an adverse reaction from his direct reports. One of his direct reports shared this story with me before leaving the organization for another career opportunity. Notice what went terribly wrong in terms of recognition and praise.

The story starts when the new library director called a special meeting for his thirty-one-member management team to talk about the new strategic goals and vision for the library. The narrator of the story noted that everyone was on edge before the meeting because the organization had been suffering from low staff morale, apathy, and high turnover. The managers were hopeful that the new director would chart a new and positive course for improving workplace culture. After everyone assembled in the boardroom, the new director started the meeting by going over his own impressive accomplishments. He revealed that the secret to his success was to never be happy or satisfied at work. By never being happy or satisfied and keeping everyone on edge, complacency would never become a threat or even a possibility. He explained that there would be very few "pats on the back" for good or great work because there is always room for improvement, and too much praise makes people lazy. The director finally announced that all managers would receive "performance expectation memos" that would be added to their personnel files. He smiled as he said that too many of these memos would result in termination, which should push everyone to do their best. The director concluded by strongly suggesting that the managers should use this "performance expectation memos" strategy with their own direct reports for maximum performance. Pleased with his speech and not taking questions, he thanked them for a great meeting and then headed out the door.

Because he was reading from notes, the library director did not notice the verbal and nonverbal cues from his management team. After the meeting, everyone was silent for several minutes before quietly exiting the boardroom to head out for lunch. During lunch, a few library managers talked about retirement. Others were comparing strategies to stay under the radar and not make any waves until the new director left for another job. The narrator of the story, realizing that he was not close to retirement and could not hide from the library director, knew that it was time to start actively looking for another job.

The library director truly felt that he was providing a motivating speech to improve workplace performance. The problem is that not only did he say he was not going to praise or recognize their efforts (belonging, esteem), but he also threatened their jobs through mandatory expectation memos (safety, security). Threatening managers with the loss of their security and safety is not going to motivate them to pursue self-actualization (which is actually what the director wanted from all his employees). Eventually, with little or no positive recognition and not-so-subtle threats of losing their job, the managers in this example were determined to stay under the radar (become disengaged) or, in the case of the narrator, look for another position.

EMPLOYEE ENGAGEMENT THROUGH POSITIVE RECOGNITION

Almost all employee engagement studies have found that in order for employees to find purpose and meaning in their work, they need frequent validation and recognition that tie into the greater goals of the organization (Schwantes 2018). This validation and recognition can come from anyone in the organization, but research suggests that it has the most impact when it comes from either your direct supervisor or the CEO of the organization. The following section illustrates what happened when a CEO—or in this case, the former director of the Broward County Library system—got involved with recognizing individuals and in many cases left a lifelong impression.

A Story about Sam: Positive Recognition and Praise

When I first started work as a regional library manager in Broward County (part of the Miami metro area in Florida), one of my first courses of action was to conduct a multitude of site visits to get to know the staff at the different libraries. As I visited each library and casually asked questions about workplace culture, a pattern and certain stories emerged from long-term employees. Staffers loved sitting down with me and telling a "Sam Morrison" story. These stories were about a time when the library organization felt like a team, and everyone supported each other and celebrated each other's wins.

They credited the family environment to the former director of the Broward County Library system, Sam Morrison, who excelled at making people feel special. Although each person was quick to let me know that things had not been perfect and the organization had problems, they all agreed that Sam Morrison sincerely cared about people. Many of their personal stories were about how the library director stopped by the library and spent some time shelving or checking out books, sitting at the reference desk, or reading to children. Sam often sent a handwritten note expressing concern about your sick grandmother or congratulating you for approaching an old problem with a fresh perspective. One librarian sat down and told me how she'd been a library shelver when Sam walked into the library and started shelving books. As they talked, Sam noticed that the shelver knew how to engage with the children in the area, and so he encouraged her to become a children's librarian. So, over the next six years, the shelver took advantage of the educational opportunities in Broward County to complete her bachelor's degree and then obtain an MLIS degree with a concentration in children's services. For each step of the way, Sam would send a quick note congratulating her on her progress toward the final goal. After getting her MLIS, the children's librarian, who is now a library manager, showed me Sam's letters, which she kept proudly on her bookcase. Another supervisor (now a Friend of the Library) was eager to tell me her story about her interactions with Sam before she retired. She said that one day she casually mentioned to Sam that she was taking ballroom dancing classes to gain more confidence in social settings. Well, several months later at a library retirement party, once the music started, Sam walked right over to the supervisor and asked her to dance, to the envy of all her colleagues. Although this dance had occurred nineteen years ago, she had a twinkle in her eye and talked about the experience as if it had happened last week. Everyone remarked that Sam Morrison was a busy man, but he was never so important that he couldn't spend time with his employees. Today, Sam Morrison still lives in the community, and even after being retired for seventeen years, he is still a popular guest at all library-related parties. People come up to him like he was a rock star, although he is a noticeably quiet and unassuming man. At the African-American Research Library and Cultural Center (in Fort Lauderdale), there is an animatronic display dedicated to his passion and his commitment to making a difference.

The stories people tell about Sam Morrison are consistent with employee recognition research. Sam took the time to recognize his staff members, and it was the little things he did that made a big difference. His handwritten letters from twenty years ago are still showcased, and not many have forgotten his acts of kindness. Everyone recognized that he was a busy man, but that is why his simple acts made such a lasting impression. It is also important to note that this did not mean the organization was perfect or free of problems, but when leadership shows that it genuinely cares, people are willing to overlook mistakes.

RECOGNITION AND PRAISE: RECOMMENDATIONS

- *Set up a plan or strategy for recognition and praise.* It can be more informal, but there needs to be a strategy. Direct supervisors who have plenty of direct contacts can incorporate positive feedback in the "check-in" meetings. If direct supervisors are more remote, then they should actively find time to set formal meetings to talk about process and provide timely feedback. It is important to always focus on what you want, not on what you do not want, when it comes to feedback.
- *Take some time and review various peer recognition programs.* Not all of these programs are created equal, so start a task force or committee that is willing to look at a variety of options and pick one that works for your organization. Peer recognition programs are a wonderful way to start a culture of continuous positive feedback, but it takes time, focus, and effort to get this right.
- *Read up on reinforcement theory and behavioral analysis.* I cannot stress enough the importance of positive and negative reinforcement and

their impact on employee morale. This is not to say you cannot give any negative feedback, nor should managers praise substandard performance, but we need to understand how behavioral theory works and be more conscious of the effect our actions can have on employee morale.

- *Take some time to see who is being rewarded in group settings.* My interviews with staff show that more extroverted employees who are confident about their accomplishments tend to get the attention, while more introverted employees who do more technical tasks or background work are ignored.

- If your organization lacks the funds to do elaborate recognition programs, remember the Sam Morrison rule: *true acts of kindness and recognition go a long way.*

INTERVIEW WITH
Jamar O. Rahming, Library Director

Jamar O. Rahming is the director of the Wilmington Public Library in Delaware. Jamar and his administrative team oversee the running of the Wilmington Library and the North Wilmington Branch Library. Each library has teams of library professionals, support staff, and volunteers who work to provide quality community service and innovative programming for their customers.

Jamar came highly recommended from a friend who attended a few of the Wilmington Public Library's amazing programs. She said the library is lovely and they always recruit exciting artists, authors, and musicians. I looked at Jamar's LinkedIn profile and the programs were stellar, so I contacted him for an interview. During our conversation I found Jamar to be responsive, approachable, and truly knowledgeable about the Wilmington community, local politics, and how to inspire and motivate his organization. His answers were so filled with common sense that I kept smiling and nodding throughout the interview.

Jamar shared the secret to his success—recognize good talent, trust your employees, remove obstacles and barriers, and then get out of your staff's way.

As a new library director, what recommendations would you give for someone to start a positive workplace culture campaign?

The first thing a new library director needs to do is to start with a vision and communicate the vision clearly. Then I encourage people to come together and provide strategies and solutions on the journey to accomplishing the organizational goals. Recognize your employees for their good work, and in turn you will get a better result. People love being recognized for doing a great job, so it is important to make sure the staff feel valued. Trust that the staff have the expertise and commitment to come up with great solutions. In terms of celebrations of great ideas and accomplishments, I unabashedly bring in food.

As a new library director, what recommendations would you suggest for building trust?

I started traditionally by having an open-door policy and listening to my staff and administrative team. But the key to building and strengthening trust is to trust your employees. If you don't trust your staff, they will not trust management. Most staff come to work wanting to do their best and feel valued for their accomplishments. If you understand this basic concept and encourage staff to solve problems and work together, you are halfway there to turning things around.

How does your organization handle conflict? How did you work with staff members who may be resistant to change?

I am lucky that the library staff have been together for years, so they are like a family. We rarely have major conflicts, but when something comes up, we try our best to resolve things directly without it escalating to major problems. I find that the best strategy is to just listen. So, I listen, do not interrupt, and stay engaged.

In the course of encouraging teamwork, collaboration, and innovation, have you seen any changes that would positively impact your customers?

Trust your employees. Let your employees know that we want to inspire, delight, and engage our customers, and then trust that the employees will come up with great solutions. My job is to provide financial and other resources to make these ideas a reality. For creativity and innovation, you must be willing to sometimes fall on your face in order to inspire progress. It first starts with your being willing to make mistakes. Owning up to your mistakes encourages others to do the same.

I was surprised that you were able to eliminate performance reviews. Are you doing quarterly reviews, or how are you providing crucial feedback to your employees?

I am lucky because our organization is a 501(c)(3), which allows more flexibility to make decisions. I found that the annual performance review was ineffective and did not encourage relationship-building. So, we have goals, but it is more about supervisors working with employees to inspire individual performance and resolve problems immediately. It is all about relationship-building and forming partnerships with our staff. We wanted fewer barriers to working as a team and making staffers feel valued and inspired for their individual contributions. By recognizing the employees for their hard work, and making sure they know you are there to remove barriers and serve as their champion, I find that staff are motivated to do their best. Trust people and then get out of their way. ■ ■ ■

REFERENCES

Hopper, Elizabeth. 2019. "Maslow's Hierarchy of Needs Explained." February 25. ThoughtCo. www.thoughtco.com/maslows-hierarchy-of-needs-4582571.

Schwantes, Marcel. 2018. "What Do Employees Want from Their Bosses, Exactly? This Study Sums It Up in 1 Simple Sentence." March 7. *Inc.* www.inc.com/marcel-schwantes/what-do-employees-want-from-their-bosses-exactly-this-study-sums-it-up-in-1-simple-sentence.html.

Feedback and Performance Evaluation

et's face it, almost everyone dreads the annual review and the overall performance evaluation process. Even in the best of times, giving feedback is hard, and if it is done only once a year, it sometimes feels perfunctory rather than constructive and supportive. However, if you get this area wrong, the organization's star employees can quickly become disengaged or disgruntled. To combat this, experts in employee engagement trends are moving away from structured annual reviews to less formal one-on-one conversations. This performance management trend sees feedback as involving more two-way communication and just-in-time continuous feedback so the employee knows where they stand. The rationale for eliminating annual reviews is that the performance evaluation model is not only time-consuming, but it often focuses on outdated goals that do not capture timely employee contributions. With continuous feedback, the focus is on just-in-time feedback and more conversations throughout the year instead of an uncomfortable yearly meeting. Continuous feedback also provides more formal opportunities for positive reinforcement, which is what improves morale in the workplace.

Research has shown that continuous feedback is seen as overwhelmingly positive and can be more effective than an annual review in motivating staff and encouraging more creativity and innovation (Cappelli and Tavis 2016). When there is a good flow of communication, the quality of work can improve from average to excellent (Weinstein 2016). Companies are now working with employees' strengths and talents to help guide them through more achievable small wins. By focusing on smaller, more obtainable wins and meeting more frequently, organizations are getting more accomplished and employees are not going too far off track before receiving feedback. This is where feedback, recognition, and praise all work together toward more positive reinforcement.

TRADITIONAL ANNUAL REVIEWS: STORIES FROM THE TRENCHES

The following case studies are real stories from library employees who had to make tough decisions based on performance appraisals. In both cases, the annual reviews resulted in negative reinforcement, and in the second case, penalty and punishment as well. In both situations, the administration was not aware of the actions and the effects they were having on their employees until it was too late.

CASE STUDY 1

Counterpunch Annual Reviews Result in Legal Action

In this first case study, a new academic librarian has consulted a lawyer as he weighs his options after a series of events that left him upset. Potentially suing your employer is serious business, so I wanted to relay this story without revealing names or the location.

The academic librarian currently works for a tenure-track organization. The performance appraisals are structured so that the employee receives a traditional annual review for the first two years, but in the third year the person receives a pre-tenure evaluation. Based on the outcome of the pre-tenure evaluation, the employee is either recommended to move forward in the tenure process or receives a "probation status" until the pre-tenure qualifications are met. If the person cannot meet the pre-tenure qualifications after the probation period, the yearly contract will not be extended.

When the new librarian arrived on the job, he was told by his colleagues that approximately 30 percent of new employees were put on probation and only 50 percent of junior faculty receive a tenure appointment. Determined to do a good job, in his first year the new librarian worked tirelessly above and beyond the call of duty to stand out from the crowd. His immediate supervisor only met with him quarterly for approximately thirty minutes. At the time, the librarian thought the limited time was normal and that "no news is good news" in terms of performance feedback. Before his annual review, he was required to write down all his accomplishments and his potential goals for next year. After reviewing his document, he was pleased with it and was looking forward to an excellent first-year review. Unfortunately, he was in for a total shock when he sat down with his supervisor and read a very lukewarm review. His accomplishments had been turned into a sort of "point/counterpoint." So, the new document read like "the librarian designed a popular information literacy video, but was commonly late to the reference desk," and "the librarian was selected for a national committee, but was turned down for a campus task force." When the librarian asked his supervisor how he could improve his performance for the following year, he was told that the document provided clear direction.

So, the following year, the librarian worked even harder to prove that his work was not lackluster and that he deserved an excellent second-year review. He did request to meet more frequently with his boss, but many of these meetings were canceled. By the end of the second year, the librarian had doubled the amount of his achievements and added some positive customer feedback and extra accolades in the document. Yet, just like last time, the second-year review noted all his achievements and accolades, but with counterpoints that he felt invalidated his accomplishments. This time around he was frustrated and angry, which resulted in a tense and aggressive confrontation. The supervisor pushed back and informed him that the library administration supported the review and his outburst would be noted in the next review. Looking for advice, he finally talked to more senior work colleagues. These colleagues informed him that his direct supervisor was a "tough grader" and believed in balanced evaluations with an equal amount of good and bad, so it was a toss-up for tenure. What should have provided comfort to the librarian ended up making him feel helpless, stressed, and disengaged instead of rewarding him for going the extra mile. Ironically, though, with his apparent slide in performance, his supervisor called a mandatory meeting to talk about his negative attitude at work. Seeing the writing on the wall, the librarian decided to call his family's attorney and pursue legal action.

Annual Review Dilemma for a New Library Manager

The second real-life case study looks at performance review management from a new manager's perspective. The new public library manager had been a children's librarian for five years before she was promoted to be the library manager at her local branch. After one year and several grievances later, the librarian left the library and is now at the local children's museum as the head of innovative experiences. She reached out to me on LinkedIn to tell me her story of why she left the library profession for good.

Her promotion to branch manager came as a shock. After accepting the job, she was sent to several mandatory leadership and management classes. These classes provided guidelines on how to handle problem employees and use progressive discipline. The children's librarian, who enjoyed story-times, innovative team programming, and community outreach, was not as comfortable with potential personnel problems, and so she strived for harmony in the workplace. The previous manager of the branch library had left suddenly without notice, and it was rumored that she had been forced into early retirement. Although these new things seemed scary, the new library manager enjoyed working at the branch, and the staff were a close-knit group that worked well together.

This all changed a few months later when the administrative board asked to meet with her. At the meeting, they informed her that the previous branch manager had been strongly urged to retire because she was not addressing some outstanding personnel problems. The board informed the new library manager that three of her staff members had complained about building issues to a local politician, and this insubordinate behavior would not be tolerated. The new library manager was shocked because the insubordinate employees were some of her more productive employees and were deeply passionate about serving the local community. The new manager was told that the former manager had never turned in their performance evaluations, and now it was her job to write the reviews using some language that had been provided in a separate document. The new manager read the "language" and realized that it was borderline threatening, with strong undertones that the three employees were on the hot seat for "performance issues." The manager asked if the issue of talking to politicians had been addressed after the incident, and she was told that they had all been given reprimands nine months ago and these had been placed in their personnel files. She then asked if the behavior had continued, and everyone shook their head and said no, but the language on their performance review should document the past indiscretions and reinforce the seriousness of the matter.

Feeling uncomfortable with this strategy, the new manager reached out to the retired branch manager, who informed her that a politician had an event at the library and saw mold and water leaks in the building. The politician approached the staff employees about the building issues. The staff, not knowing the protocol, answered truthfully and the politician mentioned the problem on television, which led to the library administration feeling blindsided and embarrassed. The library administration had known about the mold and water leaks, but it was not a high priority—until the negative television coverage forced them to immediately take care of the problem. The library administration felt that the staff had done this on purpose and therefore needed tough lessons. The staff were traumatized yet were finally working through the reprimands, so an annual review with more strong language and hints of dismissal would lead to unhappy, disengaged employees. So, the retired librarian had put her foot down and said no, which resulted in intense pressure for an early retirement.

Unfortunately, the new library manager was faced with the same dilemma and knew that the outcomes would lead to low morale and a drop in productivity at her branch. The library administration let her know that if she didn't comply with adding the language to the review, she would be subject to disciplinary action that could lead to her dismissal. To make matters worse, the library administrative board scheduled weekly meetings with her to monitor her progress with the annual reviews and would write her up until she complied with the requests. The new library manager became depressed under the pressure, and her family began to urge her to seek other employment options. When a position as the head of innovation opened at the local children's museum, she immediately interviewed and, when offered the position, resigned immediately from the library.

Takeaways

In both of these cases, the annual review or evaluation discouraged two-way communication and treated employees providing feedback as an act of insubordination. For instance, in the first case study, after the second lukewarm annual review, the employee became upset and was told that his "outburst" was going to be noted in his next review. In the second case study, the library manager was strongly urged to use the performance evaluation as a tool to continue to discipline the staffers nine months after the incident. When the manager disagreed with this option as a motivational tool for otherwise productively engaged employees, she was threatened with disciplinary action to gain her compliance. Although I would say that these cases are isolated incidents, too often similar stories have emerged from employees nationwide who have come to dread the annual performance review.

THE ORIGINS OF PERFORMANCE APPRAISALS

Performance appraisals can be traced back to the U.S. military's merit system, "which was created in World War I to identify poor performers for discharge or transfer" (Cappelli 2016). These performance rating systems were adopted in the corporate world because initially companies were faced with more talented employees than positions, so the appraisal system was designed to fire average or underperforming workers and not be sued for discrimination. The performance ratings were also used to protect companies from lawsuits because they could use the ratings and evaluative summaries as proof of poor performance. In the real-life stories above, you can see how the performance appraisals were not used to develop and support the employees, but to document their previous performance and protect the library from potential lawsuits. These cases show that lukewarm or negative performance reviews, especially if they are undeserved, can seriously damage morale and increase disengagement.

Traditional performance appraisals did temporarily change in the 1960s and 1970s because of a management and leadership shortage, which caused many organizations to reevaluate the review for promoting employees to leadership positions. During this time, more goal-setting and developmental tools were implemented to help new managers and leaders take on more responsibility and succeed at their supervisory roles. The performance appraisal was also used as a measurement to provide financial rewards like bonuses and raises, which were dependent on the ratings and overall score (Cappelli 2016).

Today, the trend in employee engagement is to figure out ways to use the performance evaluation as a tool to monitor the progress and development of the employee. This is accomplished by increasing the number of interactions between employees and their direct supervisors so that the evaluation process is more of an evolving partnership instead of a way to document past performance. Other organizations have eliminated the annual reviews altogether and instead offer monthly check-ins and more frequent conversations; this creates more opportunities to make sure that everyone is on the same page as they progress during the year. This is crucial because the most common criticism of annual performance appraisals is that they are designed to document the performance and goals for the past year. This strategy has been proven to not be as relevant because organizations and companies sometimes must adapt to new information quickly and modify their practices accordingly. For instance, no one would have predicted in 2019 that the world would be facing a global pandemic and many people would be working remotely, without face-to-face customer interactions.

EASY-TO-IMPLEMENT STRATEGIES TO IMPROVE PERFORMANCE MANAGEMENT

1. *Create clear expectations*—Most employees feel they do not know exactly what is expected of them throughout the year. To start a new year, sit down and not only talk about expectations, but also a plan to stay flexible. Today's organizations must be able to adapt to constant change. Employees who not only know the expectations but feel confident that they can accomplish the goals will have a better sense of accomplishment.
2. *Work together on big-picture goals and objectives*—Employees should always know how their goals fit in with the big-picture goals and objectives of the organization. People need to know how they fit into the larger organization and how their position is valuable to the overall goals of the institution.

3. *Frequent feedback*—Instead of yearly feedback, schedule both formal and informal meetings with staff members. During these meetings, there can be more formal conversations, but sometimes it is just a time for informal discussions. For managers, frequent meetings allow more opportunities for positive reinforcement, where they are telling employees what they are doing right and providing ways for them to continue this behavior.

4. *Focus on current accomplishments along with future development*— During both the formal and informal meetings, this is the time to talk about where the organization is going and solicit creative and innovative ideas. Because the employees and direct supervisors are meeting more often, the employee has time to reflect during their daily activities and provide ideas throughout the year.

5. *Work together on static standardized forms*—One complaint I commonly hear is that the larger organization or institution has a standardized evaluation form or process that cannot be changed. This is okay because with more frequent meetings and a better understanding of the employee through informal discussions, you can work on the traditional evaluation forms together. That way, the person has a better idea of where they stand and where they need to improve, so there should be no surprises.

HOW TO GIVE CONSTRUCTIVE FEEDBACK: APPRECIATIVE INQUIRY

Giving feedback is hard, but providing constructive feedback can make even the best of us feel uncomfortable. Many supervisors avoid it altogether, or wait until it is down in writing at an annual review to deliver bad news. There has been a lot written about appreciative inquiry, and when I talked to corporations nationwide, they were using some form of inquiry to enhance communications. Appreciative, positive feedback can serve as a powerful motivator when it provides specific suggestions on what to improve and what the person is doing well and needs to continue doing. Let's take a look at how to give both positive and constructive feedback.

Some suggestions on appreciative feedback include:

- Recognizing the specific behavior that you want to positively rein-force—*"Nancy, I appreciated the way you looked for alternative solutions to secure the talent for our event. Your quick thinking and innovation saved the day."*
- Stress the potential impact the behavior had on the organization or team—*"Charles, your interactive presentation at today's meeting was excellent. The stakeholders were impressed, and it was due in part to your taking the time to work through the details."*
- Engage in positive reinforcement to enhance and strengthen the behavior that you want to see continue—*"Pearl, you are an excellent researcher and have been getting reports to me in record time; keep up the good work!"* (Douglas 2018).

Constructive feedback is sometimes unavoidable, but even in these situations, appreciative feedback can be used to defuse a defensive reaction or keep the person from shutting down and not receiving the guidance. Benedictine University has an excellent article on how to approach con-structive feedback. The article highlights a three-step system that focuses on opportunities to provide positive reinforcement:

Step 1: *Identify the problem, challenge, or opportunity for improvement.* For instance, you noticed that attendance at the Instructional Services Department's classes is down by 20 percent, and so you approach Janice, the department head of Instructional Services, for answers.

Step 2: *Reframe the problem as a future opportunity.* Instead of blurting out that the department's attendance numbers are down and if they are not brought up soon, you'll hold Janice accountable . . . inform her that one of the library's strengths is the Instructional Services Department, so you want to work with her on exceeding expectations and devising a strategy to make this happen.

Step 3: *Identify what has made success possible in the past.* This is where you reinforce specific behaviors that you think will contribute to solving the problem or overcoming the obstacle. For example, in this instance, you can talk about how honestly impressed you are with Janice's ability to pull the other instructors together and find creative and innovative solutions to problems, and you are looking forward to working with her in the effort to take the Instructional Services Department to the next level (Johnson 2017).

PERFORMANCE EVALUATION: RECOMMENDATIONS

The following are some summary recommendations from libraries and corporate organizations on easy ways to develop better feedback and performance evaluation strategies at your library. As you can see, many of these strategies use positive reinforcement tools to reward individual contributions.

- Develop a formal plan where managers and supervisors meet with their staff regularly. The meeting themselves do not need to be formal, but the time should be consistent. Get into a rhythm where employees and managers are having more natural conversations to solve problems, remove obstacles, and implement more positive reinforcement strategies.
- During weekly or bimonthly meetings, focus on smaller, more achievable goals. Research shows that people can become overwhelmed by long-term "stretch goals," but smaller, more achievable goals provide more opportunities for positive recognition and praise. As individuals receive more positive reinforcement for being able to accomplish goals, their confidence increases, which can lead to enhanced productivity.
- Celebrate small wins. During the weekly or biweekly meetings, when people are accomplishing smaller goals or are working successfully on a larger project, a quick celebratory congratulations to let them know they are on the right track can go a long way. Many times, organizations are in a constant state of busywork and have constant demands, so leadership rarely takes the time to reflect on the journey. Remember, what you focus on tends to grow and expand, so focus on success, not mistakes.
- In terms of feedback, consider appreciative inquiry or another tool to help people give more timely and effective feedback to employees and colleagues.
- During meetings, allow employees to take ownership of their goals and allow room for flexibility and problem-solving. One of the major complaints I heard during my informal interviews with employees is that managers and leaders will say that they allow for mistakes, but then employees feel severely punished when they state a difference of opinion. It is imperative that employees have an environment that allows them to try new things and not feel penalized for taking risks.

- If the library is required to have the annual review, do not use this as a vehicle for negative reinforcement. Waiting for the annual review to shock the employee with bad news is bad for business and for employee morale. The employee should never be taken by surprise by the review. Negative reinforcement with the absence of positive reinforcement lowers morale and engagement.
- The more that employees feel that the organization has their back and that management's feedback is a tool to make them more successful in the workforce, the better their overall performance will be.

SUCCESS STORIES

Although there are many sad tales about feedback and performance appraisals, several libraries have been actively working on creating a healthier climate to provide continuous feedback and more productive annual appraisals. The following three stories are from vastly different libraries, each with a different perspective and approach.

INTERVIEW WITH
Ashley Rosener, Liaison Librarian

Ashley Rosener is a liaison librarian in the professional programs at Grand Valley State University Libraries in Michigan. Her research interests include professional development in libraries, mentoring, and scholarly communications.

My research led me to Ashley's article "Leading from the Center: Reimagining Feedback Conversations at an Academic Library" (Rosener et al. 2019). The article focuses on a team of University Libraries faculty and staff who created a series of professional development workshops to strengthen the library staff's communication skills as they relate to giving and receiving feedback. The foundation for the training was appreciative inquiry, which allows for affirmative and positive questions that build trust through empathy, accountability, and resiliency. Grand Valley State University Libraries will incorporate these workshops on strengthening communication skills into all of its ongoing and future DEI efforts, thus potentially providing a strong foundation for future success.

Ashley explained to me that a committee which included library staff designed a series of "Thanks for the Feedback" task force workshops for the

University Libraries. The task force, which was focused on organizational development/change management, created peer-led workshops with support from the leadership team. One of the tools that the task force utilized was appreciative inquiry. Appreciative inquiry was initially suggested and ultimately facilitated by the new library dean, Annie Bélanger. The "Thanks for the Feedback" task force also drew upon the book *Thanks for the Feedback: The Science and Art of Receiving Feedback Well*, by Douglas Stone and Sheila Heen.

How did you initially determine who participated in the "Thanks for the Feedback" task force? Did the person need to have presentation and training skills or an interest in organizational change?

Individuals were asked if they would like to participate based on their interest and skill set. There was also a desire for representation of both faculty and staff. Most members had taken part in the appreciative inquiry.

Did your managers or leadership team receive any additional training, or were they in the same classes as the faculty and staff members?

No, they were in the same workshops alongside all faculty and staff.

Were the workshops eventually mandatory for all library faculty and staff? Did you have anyone who refused to take the training? Could managers and the leadership team opt out of the training?

The first training on interpersonal effectiveness was mandatory (and there were multiple times to attend, with options for alternative meetings if the scheduling did not work out). The subsequent feedback workshops were not mandatory, so managers and the leadership team could opt out of this training, as could staff members.

Has the training affected the way you have conducted the job recruitment process?

We now approach hiring with more empathy and an inclusive framework. We provide clear instructions and try to answer any potential questions as we work through the process. To support candidates, interview questions are shared with the candidate ahead of time. Additionally, in our job ads, we place an emphasis on the interpersonal skills required for the position.

Have you noticed a significant difference in your interpersonal communications over the past two years?

There is a greater focus on the importance of feedback, both giving it frequently and constructively and receiving it well. Interpersonal work relationships have positively grown as communication has improved. There is more accountability now to reinforce positive communication, and we have coaching plans and professional growth plans to scaffold professional development. We are norming the giving of formative feedback during our annual review process and are making sure individuals include both the how and what of their work and how it all relates to our workplace values. We also recognize that the trainings were only the start of ongoing efforts. We continue to provide training for library employees, such as trainings on both microaggressions and accessibility issues this past August during a library-wide convocation.

What are some of the DEI initiatives that you will be working on in the upcoming year?

Our library's IDEA (Inclusion, Diversity, Equity, and Accessibility) committee is working to compile a list of university inclusion and equity workshops, to create a calendar of heritage months and library user engagement activities, and to develop planning with accessibility in mind. We also continue to bring faculty fellows to our library in partnership with the ACRL's Diversity Alliance program, which unites academic libraries committed to enlarging the hiring pipeline for qualified and talented individuals from underrepresented racial and ethnic groups. Additionally, we are starting a task force to examine student hiring and retention more inclusively. ■ ■ ■

INTERVIEW WITH
Doug Crane, Library System Director

Doug Crane is the director of the Palm Beach County Library System in Florida. He is originally from Toronto, Canada, where he earned undergraduate degrees in history and geography and his MLS from the University of Toronto. Doug came to the Palm Beach County Library System in 1998 as a youth services librarian and is currently the owner of the popular blog, *The Efficient Librarian*.

My interview with Doug resulted from a referral from a Palm Beach County Library staff member. The staff member had discovered that I was writing a book, and he called me to suggest his library for its recent work with positive feedback. I reached out to the library director, Doug Crane, and we were able to schedule a phone meeting for the following week. During my interview, Doug was well-prepared and methodical and was a natural connector who helped me with my research. Doug had read several books on positive workplace culture, and this knowledge was reflected in his answers.

The first thing that Doug mentioned is some library organizations are risk-averse, so they are missing opportunities for more creativity and innovation. So, to solicit new ideas, his library developed an online database (Inkling) that allows employees to suggest new ideas. Some ideas might need a follow-up call or even a committee to accomplish, but most of the ideas were able to be accomplished immediately. This celebration of small wins has gone a long way to building trust. Doug has also tried to engage employees by encouraging fun and taking a fresh look at creative and inspiring new ideas.

Could you tell us a little more about the online database (Inkling) and what your most successful implementation of a staff member's suggestion was?

Every organization has great ideas, but rarely do the employees have a forum in which to post them. Inkling is our avenue for staff members to post ideas about all sorts of different topics. After an idea is posted, other staff members can comment on the idea and have a lively discussion. Some ideas suggested in the forum have been implemented. A good example was a suggestion to standardize our loan periods to three weeks. Prior to the suggestion, loan periods varied from one week to four weeks. At three weeks, the public does not have to worry about different return times for items. After being suggested in Inkling, the idea moved through our management team and then became an official policy within a few months.

What are the top three ways your organization inspires fun and creativity?

We give our staff broad latitude to create activities and events for the public that showcase their own passions. Whether it be line dancing, gaming, or crafting, the staff can showcase their talents by leading activities for our patrons in a fun environment. A big example from the past year was a group of staff who came together on their own to create a two-day Comic Con at our Main Library. It included cosplay, comic talks, gaming, science experiments, and more! After months of planning, the event was a huge hit with the public.

Our employee recognition awards are a chance to highlight outstanding work. Employees are recognized in a ceremony and receive one day off (with pay) as an incentive for their hard work. Their accomplishments are highlighted in the staff newsletter. This process also allows us to discover hidden talent in the organization and potentially put it to use in other projects.

Our mentorship program offers staff members an opportunity to grow and develop their careers. We match people with an appropriate mentor and provide many different breakout sessions over the year. These include personality profiling tests, luncheons with senior leaders, fun tours of the library system, and a heartwarming graduation event with an inspiring speaker.

How does your organization handle conflict before it gets to the disciplinary process?

We use an approach from the SBI model. SBI stands for Situation, Behavior, and Impact. The model is a way to take the emotion out of an employee discussion and focus it on the facts. When entering into a coaching or performance meeting, the supervisors identify the situation (i.e., time/place) and describe the behavior as if it was viewed through a camera and then assess the impact of that behavior as a way to guide the employee to the appropriate action.

This process is important because it helps us focus on the specific issue and provide clear guidance on our expectations for the employee. It also creates key documentation that can be used to provide instruction memos.

The SBI process has the added benefit of providing a key opportunity for the employee to share their viewpoint. Sometimes conflicts arise from miscommunication or misunderstandings. The structured meeting provides a simple way for the staff member to share their concerns and get immediate feedback.

If a new library director or manager wanted to know how to get started inspiring a more engaged workforce, what would be your advice?

The first step is always to listen first. Often a new leader may come in with great ideas and pet projects to launch. However, if they do not take the time to learn more about their organization and connect with the people who comprise it, they may end up going in the wrong direction very quickly. Typically, there is a problem or an old way of doing things which is a pain point for staff that needs to be resolved. A new leader can show their support by tackling that issue first, and only afterward start advancing their own ideas. For example, when I became director, the staff were upset about a prior decision that forced those working on Sundays to work only a partial day and then make it up throughout the week. I reversed that decision, which simplified schedules and made many people happy right away.

In a large organization like yours, how do you make sure your managers and leadership team implement positive feedback strategies?

We are still working on our own processes and seeing opportunities for improvement. Any time an organization is spread over multiple locations and different work shifts, it can be challenging to keep everyone connected. One aspect we are exploring is how we do employee reviews. Our old system was not useful, so we stopped it. However, that meant we have no regular system for feedback. Instead, we are experimenting with new approaches. At one of our branches, the manager is working closely with all his staff to craft engaging goals tailored to each person. We are also developing our culture playbook through a committee called Firewatchers, inspired by the book *Primed to Perform*, by Lindsay McGregor and Neel Doshi. This playbook will emphasize our desired culture and then the committee will work to implement it. We plan to launch this in 2020.

What does your organization do to continue to inspire trust that the leadership team has their best interests at heart?

This is an ongoing process that is never complete. Communication is one of the keys to ensuring that people feel trusted. We recognize in our organization that we need to open the channels much wider to share news and decisions. For example, in the five years I have been director, I planned visits to each one of our locations twice a year for an hour-long session. These were opportunities to share ideas, gather feedback, and meet staff. This past year I have done workdays where I spend a half day at each location and work alongside the staff as they go about their regular duties. We also provide updates and information in our staff newsletter. The Inkling portal is also an avenue for communication with the staff, as leadership team members will comment and reply to items. ■ ■ ■

INTERVIEW WITH
Mary Jo Finch, Library Director

Mary Jo Finch is the director of the Westbank Community Library in Austin, Texas. During its thirty-six-year-long history, the library has seen many changes. Initially, the library was a nonprofit, with no regular source of income, that relied on donations and volunteerism and was housed in a spare room in the local bank. Today, the Westbank Library is a two-branch district serving about 27,000 people, with more than 250,000 visitors per year and a circulation of about 500,000 items annually.

In the course of researching libraries that have made a difference internally, I read Mary Jo's article "Antifragile Management and the End of the Annual Performance Review" (Finch and Solomon 2017). I was intrigued by an organization that had phased out the dreaded annual review but was still able to provide valuable feedback, enhance trust, and increase workplace engagement. So, after reading this excellent and insightful article, I reached out to Mary Jo to find out more information for this book. Mary Jo was fun to talk to, and what stood out for me were her patience, determination, and resilience.

Mary Jo has replaced the annual performance review with a feedback loop. The feedback loop contains one-on-one meetings and progress check-ins. During the one-on-one meetings, the employee takes the lead in the meeting by talking about both their accomplishments and concerns, with the managers providing constructive feedback, asking questions, and offering suggestions. The progress check-ins currently take place three times a year and are much longer meetings. The meetings follow a prescribed set of questions in order to delve deeper into the employee's goals, accomplishments, and next steps.

Mary Jo mentioned that trust took a while to be established and for managers and employees to begin seeing each other as partners. And as everyone knows, giving constructive feedback is hard, and it must be continually practiced like a muscle to get better. People think that positive or appreciate feedback would be easier, but everything takes practice and commitment to get better. As you read Mary Jo's interview, you will notice that she provides great advice and a strong framework for employee engagement, positive reinforcement, and common-sense advice.

Would you suggest that organizations receive formal training on how to give and receive feedback?

Training, yes, but not necessarily formal training. In all the decisions we make, we must have a goal (or goals) in mind. What is the goal of our feedback loop, and what, if any, training might help us reach that goal? At our library, the goal of our feedback conversations is for employees and managers to build a partnership that allows employees to take full responsibility for their part in running the library, with guidance from managers. We want employees to prioritize their workload, to solve problems as they arise in the course of their work, to bring new ideas, to ask for input when they need it, to assess their own progress, and to shift direction when it seems appropriate. We want employees to become good decision-makers, and we recognize and welcome mistakes as part of that process. We want managers to help employees think through those aspects of a decision they may have missed, to provide information that will be helpful, and to share advice based on experience or on the needs of the library. It is less "feedback" than it is simply conversation, though it may include requests to do something differently.

As trust is built in the employee-manager partnership, feedback becomes just a conversational exchange of information. I do think some people as individuals struggle with trust. They may be a little less forthcoming in sharing information, and they may be less inclined toward introspection. This may limit their career growth, but we have learned not to push them in conversation past their comfort level.

Did the managers receive special training to prepare them for the change in the feedback/evaluation format?

Honestly, we threw it out on the table at a managers' meeting and said, "Let's try this." We talked together about why we wanted to do it and how it would work, and we talked through the managers' reservations about the process. Then we did our first round of check-ins, and we talked about how it went. Initially, we did check-ins quarterly, but it was too much, and we revised the schedule to just three times per year.

We have six managers on our team, and we meet once or twice a month to share information, coordinate work across teams, discuss management readings, and coach each other. We are teaching ourselves as we go along with the help of a wide variety of outside readings and webinars. In the early days, we practiced conversations with each other as we worked toward asking more questions and giving less advice. We still do sometimes, but holding conversations is something we have all grown better at.

Every employee-manager partnership is unique. Some employees fully engage in the process and have so many ideas that the manager spends a lot of time helping them narrow their scope. Some employees have more structured jobs, and their one-on-ones may be short catch-ups. Some managers work alongside their employees, so their one-on-ones may be conversations during work time rather than a scheduled meeting. Some partnerships work best if the one-on-ones have a regular agenda format. A one-on-one can last anywhere from 15 minutes to 90 minutes. It might be once a week or once a month. The manager and employee must find their own rhythm and process.

The progress check-ins work similarly. The check-in is a set of questions to prompt deeper conversation, and some employees will engage with some questions and not with others. And that is okay. The point is not to push people into discomfort. It's to help the employee to set goals, to recognize their own accomplishments, to identify when a change of course is necessary, to understand their responsibilities, and to hone a job over time in a way that aligns with their personal motivations. Most managers send the questions to the employee ahead of time, and most employees bring notes to the meeting, pre-thinking what they want to talk about.

How does your organization handle conflict? Is this reflected in the feedback loop?

Conflict? What conflict? ☺ Truthfully, we have very little.

I think a large part of our success is that we set expectations up front. Our employee manual describes our antifragile management philosophy, the kind of experience we are trying to create for the community, and the work culture that is required to create that experience. The manual helps people figure out what steps to take when things are not going well. Going through the manual is part of our onboarding process, so every new employee comes on board with their expectations set.

Managers may get involved in helping to resolve occasional differences if issues are raised in one-on-ones. Sometimes there is an organizational solution to a problem, and sometimes we need to remind people to be more accepting of the differences of others, but other times the individuals involved do need to recalibrate.

The underlying principle here is "antifragility," the idea that experiencing stressors can make us stronger. We accept that sometimes folks will not agree, and when they get stuck in disagreement, we can point them to the employee manual and remind them what is expected of them. Some examples of expectations called out in the employee manual are:

- To bring a positive attitude
- To be slow to judge and quick to help out
- To look for the next best thing we can do to make a situation better
- To bring kindness, humor, and value to our work
- To consider what is best for the library in addition to our own needs
- To think beyond our job to how our work intersects with everyone else's to keep the library running smoothly

Have you seen an increase in employee engagement since you have worked on strengthening trust in the workplace? Are there any areas where you have seen significant improvement?

Absolutely! Some examples of employee-driven change are:

- Our programs team read the book *Free to Learn* (Peter Gray) and invented our own version of Free Play, which continues to grow in scope. We are now working on a grant project with Dr. Gray to examine how libraries, as centers of self-education, could become centers of learning through play. We are also developing our outdoor spaces for exploratory activity.
- A team of our librarians developed sensory programming, a special needs volunteer program, and an ASL storytime. They presented at a state conference on special needs and Free Play programming and hosted two workshops at our library.
- Our programs team has steadily grown the number and variety of programs we offer. We have added a lot more adult programs, particularly mindfulness programming for adults. The team works to balance our programming across age groups, across schedules, and across our two locations.
- As the community shifts to digital reading, physical circulations have dropped and with them, the need for people to visit the library. Visitation has increased for the second year in a row, despite continued drops in physical circulation. We get many compliments from the public about the helpfulness and friendliness of our staff.
- A public service librarian, who works side by side with many staff at the desk, noticed that some staff had "holes" in their readers' advisory (RA) repertoire, and she invented a role for herself as the RA Librarian. She does a short monthly training at staff meetings on different genres and different RA resources, she does one-on-ones and small group trainings with non-librarians who work on the desk, and she produces book lists and other PR materials about reading.
- Our new technology manager built us a beautiful website. He has developed coding and robotics programming and an arcade night.
- Two librarians (who have done Harwood training and who conducted community conversations that helped us with our strategic plan) have started doing one-on-one interviews with community leaders with the goal of finding ways to build networks and partnerships. They are also expanding our outreach endeavors.
- Our staff turnover rate has been almost nil over the last several years. It is now becoming difficult to provide a growth path for everyone, so we are shifting our hiring focus to the temporary employment of library school interns.

Realistically, how long did it take to implement the organizational changes? What would you reply to someone who says, "This sounds good, but we don't have the time or the expertise to get started"? And in retrospect, did the benefits of the changes exceed the work, time, and effort involved?

Obviously, change is a process. So, someone going into this should not think of it as a thing that gets implemented and then you just must keep it going, like you do with annual reviews.

The feedback loop is more like a living thing. If you want it to thrive, you must continue to invest in it. It is not a top-down process. It is not plug-and-play. What you are signing on to with a feedback loop like this is a collaborative process that will be shaped to your goals and your staff. Every year we revise some of the progress check-in questions in line with our focus for the year. As director, I read the notes from all employee progress check-ins each time because that is where I get the most feedback about what is on people's minds. Sometimes this results in new ideas to pursue. Also, you need to make sure managers have actual management time as well as white space for thinking.

It is hard to say how long the changes took because they're ongoing. Some employees embraced progress check-ins fully the first time around. Some took a little longer. You may have one or two people on the staff who really struggle with trust because of their own life or work history, and they may never fully embrace the process, though I have found that they do participate within their level of comfort.

For organizations that are stuck politically with their annual evaluation, what alternative ways would you suggest to get started on becoming an antifragile organization?

It helps to have a good understanding of what "antifragile" means. Simplistically, "antifragile" means growing stronger when exposed to stressors (and particularly acute stressors followed by recovery time rather than chronic stressors). Nassim Taleb wrote a 400-page book to explain the concept, so reading his book (i.e., *Antifragile: Things That Gain from Disorder*) or a good summary of it would be a great place to start.

As an organization, there are many things we can do to become more antifragile, like the following ones:

- Working in teams to allow for collaboration
- Having people work on more than one team and doing cross-training to create redundancies
- Welcoming mistakes to encourage the trial and error necessary for innovation
- Having a budget for unanticipated innovations
- Reducing rules wherever possible (our Code of Conduct has three rules: respect others, respect our property, and stay safe)
- Accepting that most rules will have exceptions, and not creating new rules to deal with exceptions
- Coaching the staff to make decisions instead of making decisions for them
- Aiming for flexibility
- Hiring people who are good at change (really think about your interview questions)
- Making safe decisions 80 percent of the time and risky decisions 20 percent of the time
- Prioritizing learning and staff development
- Encouraging play and playfulness; this is nature's way of learning to take risks, strategize, and negotiate ■ ■ ■

REFERENCES

Cappelli, P., and A. Tavis. 2016. "The Performance Management Revolution." *Harvard Business Review* 5 (October): 58–67.

Douglas, Eric. 2018. "A Balanced Approach to Giving Good Feedback." July 2. LRI: Leading Resources, Inc. https://leading-resources.com/leadership/a-balanced -approach-to-giving-good-feedback/.

Finch, Mary Jo, and Autumn Solomon. 2017. "Antifragile Management and the End of the Annual Performance Review." Public Libraries Online. http://public librariesonline.org/2017/12/antifragile-management-and-the-end-of-the -annual-performance-review.

Johnson, Amber. 2017. "Giving Appreciative Feedback: Expand Your Leadership Results." Center for Values-Driven Leadership, Benedictine University. https:// cvdl.ben.edu/blog/appreciative_feedback/.

Rosener, Ashley, et al. 2019. "Leading from the Center: Reimagining Feedback Conversations at an Academic Library." *In the Library with the Lead Pipe*. www.inthelibrarywiththeleadpipe.org/2019/reimagining-feedback.

Weinstein, Margery. 2016. "Annual Review Under Review." *Training* 53, n. 4 (April): 22–28.

Teamwork and Collaboration

O ne of the biggest drivers of employee engagement is developing a team spirit or a sense of collaboration. Teamwork is still the number-one way for getting work done—from small pilot projects to try out a new idea, to exciting strategic goals that will have maximum impact. According to a study completed by Maxwell, in the corporate world, 90 percent of businesses stated their projects are so detailed and involved that they need teams working on them (Maxwell 2007).

When we look at Maslow's "hierarchy of needs," positive teamwork and feeling like you are a part of a group directly satisfy the need for belonging and inclusion. It is natural to think that teamwork comes naturally because employees spend so much time together in the office or—in some cases— remotely through Zoom or other video communication platforms. Teamwork can lead to innovative ideas and stronger workplace performance—but it can also be stressful. When I first started my career as a librarian, I worked at the University of Arizona, which at the time was a team-based environment in which 80 percent of our work was done through work teams and cross-functional teams. What I can say is that some teams worked like magic and were lauded on a national level. However, there were also plenty of teamwork meltdowns, where an intervention was needed to get the team back on track. Without tools and strategies to handle conflict, tension, and obstacles, massive breakdowns in communication are bound to materialize. Creating an environment where the organization feels more like a family does not happen overnight, however. In this chapter, we will start by looking at high-performing teams, then look at strategies to support dysfunctional teams, and finally offer some tips on how to develop remote teamwork.

CRITERIA FOR HIGH-PERFORMING TEAMS

The *Forbes* article "13 Characteristics of a High-Performing Team" provides an excellent framework for both short-term and long-term teamwork. It is a must-read, but for this book, I will just highlight some of the criteria that are needed for people to thrive in the workplace.

1. *Know the strengths, talents, and abilities of the team*—This criterion should be both highlighted and in bold. What I find from my consultant work, when there has been a definite breakdown in team communication, is that the team didn't take the time to figure out what is needed to make the team successful and then determine if they have the right strengths on the team. This is most apparent when organizations form diversity, equity, and inclusion committees. When you talk to people about what they feel is needed to make such a committee successful, in many cases they have no idea. What happens is that people select the committee's members based on the volunteers' passion and interest and then find they need a facilitator, presenter, critical race theory expert, strong writer, or an expert collaborator. Before the teamwork starts, you should look beyond the excitement and interest and ask what is truly needed to be successful. If the volunteers for the team do not have the skills, this is the time to recruit based on what is needed.
2. *Focus on hitting a relevant goal*—Keep in mind that when you create your initial goals and objectives, this will be a fluid document because there is a definite likelihood that things may change. Take time to discover key or relevant goals that must be accomplished but try to remain flexible, depending on what you find throughout the course

of the project. Doing this allows people to change course and not get too stuck if something is not working, while still allowing them to focus on the big picture.

3. *Organize work based on the strengths of the team*—During the team-building or onboarding stage of a project, people should take some time to talk about the different strengths they bring to the project and their work style. By knowing what unique talents everyone has, the work can be divided up better to create a win/win environment. The best teams occur when each team member has a role, and feels confident that they can step up to the challenge and exceed. Work styles are important because some people are planners, while others are procrastinators who are motivated by impending deadlines. Knowing this up front and developing agreed-upon strategies to adapt to different styles can work wonders for more positive job performance.

4. *Communication, communication, communication*—This is make or break in the beginning. You cannot communicate enough until everyone is on the same page and the team is operating on all cylinders. Keep in mind that communication in this sense is not just verbal. Just as you know people's strengths, you should also know their preferred communication style and be open to communicating in writing, face-to-face, video chat, or through other communication platforms.

5. *Creating safe spaces*—Creating safe spaces ties into the importance of communication. High-performing teams try to create safe spaces for disagreement. Research has proven that some disagreement is healthy and, in some cases, necessary to challenge traditional thoughts and assumptions. However, one must draw a line between healthy differences of opinion and lively discussions on the one hand and bitter disagreements that result in hurt feelings and members shutting down on the other.

6. *Careful selection of the team leaders*—Too many times, the team leader is someone who reluctantly accepts the job because no one else wants to take the responsibility. The person who leads the project or work team can sometimes make or break future progress. Great teams take the time to determine the skill set of the team leader and select the best fit. Some possible traits to keep in mind are good facilitation skills, ability to see the big picture, skill at problem-solving, a willingness to delegate, and good people skills (*Forbes* 2016).

WHEN STRENGTHS COME TOGETHER FOR HIGH IMPACT

In my experience leading teams, being a team member, and consulting with teams, when the team elevates to a "high performing" status, it is like magic where everyone feels part of a family. It is especially great when the team encounters challenges along the way but is able to pull together and achieve a successful outcome. When I was the executive director at the African-American Research Library and Cultural Center (in Fort Lauderdale, Florida), we used to put on several high-profile cultural events, as well as two or three large-scale events every month. This heavy programming schedule, with its myriad details for planning, promotion, and execution, required high-functioning teams with clearly defined roles. Most of the logistics and initial work were carried out by an organizing committee, but the actual execution of the event was entrusted to a smaller internal work team. In this team we all had very clearly defined roles, knew what needed to get done, and after a while felt confident to handle any challenges that inevitably came our way. From the catering running behind schedule, to artists who refused to perform without coaxing, to technology glitches, and to occasional customer complaints, we trusted each other to get things done, and we made each event look easy. My job was to be "the host" handling all things people—greeting guests, hugging, dancing, taking photos with new and loyal customers, and fending off potential complaints before they turned into a problem. My assistant had her checklist for handling all things logistical and putting out fires before anyone noticed. The head of programming worked with the catering staff, cleaning crew, and talent. We even had staff who pitched in as musicians, dance instructors, and presenters at a moment's notice if needed. At the end of the night, after our patrons had left happy, we smiled to ourselves that we had put out all the fires without looking too frazzled and that people left happy, and then we congratulated ourselves on another job well done.

This high-performing work team did not materialize overnight, and it took some time and trial and error to get it right. It took us some time to understand how each member of the work team complemented each other, and gradually we developed trust that the other person would execute their role for a common goal. As we celebrated our successes and stayed flexible, each "win" helped solidify our connection to our work.

THE FIVE DYSFUNCTIONS OF A TEAM

Good teamwork can result in more engagement because it reinforces the individual strengths and abilities that people bring to the organization. One friend said that teamwork is like a boss: when it's good, it is really good, but when it's bad, it can erode one's well-being. Dysfunction in teams, if not properly addressed, can lead to stress, low job satisfaction, low engagement, poor productivity, anger, and eventually personnel turnover.

All teams will, at one time or another, face the challenge of fostering harmony in groups. According to Patrick Lencioni, author of a popular book on team dynamics, *The Five Dysfunctions of a Team,* human beings are inherently dysfunctional (Lencioni 2011). Therefore, leaders must recognize and drive groups to overcome certain behavioral tendencies, many of which are negative and can bring down an entire organization.

Organizations often put a lot of thought into organizing teams and *getting them up and running*. But a team is an ongoing social unit that requires a lot of care and maintenance to ensure that it keeps performing effectively. While regular check-ins and team-building exercises are a good way to ensure that team members have the skills and relationships necessary for productive collaboration, leaders should always be on the lookout for behaviors that serve as clear warning signs of a dysfunctional team, both in-person and in a virtual environment.

Think back to teams that you were on. If you're like many, you can recall teams that never got anything done, where backstabbing or passive-aggressive conflicts were common. Many of these dysfunctions can be remedied by team-building and adequate preparation in the beginning. Although it's sometimes a pain to do this work, and it's more exciting to just dive in and get started, careful planning and taking time to understand who is on the team and define their roles can make all the difference in avoiding Lencioni's five dysfunctions. These are:

1. *Absence of trust*—Trust is the most important element of any team, so it's no surprise that many of the warning signs (of dysfunctionality) are related to low levels of trust in some way. When team members do not trust one another, they typically respond defensively, exhibiting several detrimental behaviors that, in one way or another, are designed to protect themselves.

2. *Fear of conflict*—Fear of conflict emerges when there is no trust because people will then be unable to engage in an honest and passionate debate of ideas. The failure to vent relevant frustrations and argue intelligently results in guarded comments and unproductive discussions.

3. *Lack of commitment*—A lack of commitment prevents group members from buying into decisions because they have failed at open debate and the consideration of individual ideas. Instead of engaging in harmonious discussion, people are pretending to get along to avoid conflict.

4. *Breakdown in communication*—This usually happens once the team members do not feel there is a safe space to express their ideas. If people are pretending to get along and are not really engaging in the process, the team starts to unravel.

5. *Individual goals instead of team goals*—This occurs when team members put their own needs before those of the organization, whether those needs are career status, recognition, or financial rewards. For better team performance, there needs to be a steady focus on common goals (Lencioni 2011).

In my previous example of highly productive teams, I mentioned that it took some time to develop and strengthen trust and respect for our individual strengths. When we first started our intense work on holding public events, I noticed that some of the team members were planners and others were motivated by a "trial by fire" approach where the excitement of the unknown was the motivator. A conflict arose because I was a planner and strategic thinker, while my assistant director thrived on trial-by-fire situations. So, honestly, we clashed several times because when I was working with her on the program "plans," she appeared to be listening to me, but she really ignored me until the day of the event. During the day of the event, everything that I had recommended to do weeks ago had been ignored by her, and so instead we ran around frantically getting things done, which drove me and other "planning" project team members crazy. So, as the project team manager, I had to figure out a compromise in order for everyone to work more efficiently. Accordingly, we sat down and had an honest disussion on our different work styles and how we could work more harmoniously. The conclusion was that I would trust my assistant and other members who were more comfortable with "trials by fire" and acknowledge that their efforts always worked out in the end. And in turn more strategic planners like me would reach out to the group if we noticed obstacles that could not be resolved on the day of the event. That way, planners like me felt more comfortable that there would not be too many surprises during the event. After noticing that this worked for everyone and made our events run more smoothly, we moved from bickering with each other to admiring each other's role in our succesful programming adventures.

HOW TO COLLABORATE EFFECTIVELY IF THE TEAM IS REMOTE

Since the pandemic began, I have fielded questions on how to create team-building and collaboration in a remote or virtual environment. As some people have observed, remote work adds an additional layer of complexity to effective communication. In today's remote environment, there are few opportunities to pop into someone's cubicle and ask a quick question or solicit advice. Now, and more than ever before, technology is connecting us to our colleagues, employees, and bosses, and so creative ways to enhance communication are critical. After researching corporations and start-up companies that are all-virtual, I can offer some common-sense tips from the experts:

Engage in clear communication—This may seem like a no-brainer, but many times with virtual communication, we tend to not write in complete sentences, or we provide quick thoughts and use abbreviations. This can easily lead to people misinterpreting what you're trying to say, and using the wrong words can lead to misunderstandings. The advice here is to always check to see if the group is clear on potential goals or outcomes, and always stress feedback and encourage questions.

Develop communication norms—Some people enjoy short, to-the-point messages; others want longer messages with detailed instructions. Some people need face-to-face interaction through video chat, while others would rather talk on the phone. When working on a team, there is probably no one size fits all, but this is where understanding your team members' strengths and work styles, and whether they are extroverted or introverted, is important. Make sure that everyone is on the same page on how to communicate, how often, and in what medium so that everyone stays engaged.

Strongly encourage active engagement—Especially for teamwork, it is crucial to have some form of video communication so that everyone can receive both verbal and nonverbal cues. When working from home or remotely, it is easy to get distracted or disengaged, but when it comes to teamwork, everyone needs to be actively participating. If the teamwork requires decision-making or team-building on a larger project, people need to be present, contributing, and taking an active part in decision-making.

Allow for fun and rapport—Almost every virtual company I talked to said that it is important to set aside time for virtual happy hours, birthday celebrations, consistent recognition for a job well done, and fun activities to relax. It's easy to get meeting fatigue, and it's hard to feel connected while working from home, so it's up to the team to schedule some time and develop activities to relax and get to continuously know each other.

TEAMWORK AND COLLABORATION: RECOMMENDATIONS

The research on teamwork and collaboration stresses the value of recognizing the individual strengths that each team member brings to the table:

- When possible, have employees take a strength-based survey or test so that you can see how everyone fits together on the team. If not a survey, take the time to find out about each team member's strengths, abilities, and work style. Go beyond the job description and find out who is good with details, who challenges new ideas, who loves talking and collaborating with people, who is the best writer, who is the planner, and who is the procrastinator. The more you know up front, the easier it is to distribute the work to the greatest effect.
- Develop a document with guidelines on how to handle conflict and stress in the workplace. These guidelines need to stay fluid and can and should be updated. Spend extra time learning how to work through conflict and differences of opinion. Organizations that are consistently good at teamwork have team leaders who are trained and comfortable working through all forms of conflict, including

underperformance, disengagement, perfectionism, delegation, and tension between team members.

- Develop a quick and easy process for team-building. The team-building guidelines should be implemented for all new and current teams for consistency. These guidelines should be easy to understand, with multiple options and clear instructions.
- Invest in strategies on how to give and receive feedback.
- Celebrate both small and large wins. Create a culture where peer recognition and praise are encouraged.
- Be patient. Building high-producing teams takes time and patience. Don't beat yourself up if there are stumbles along the way.
- Consider investing in a corporate care program where employees get together and work in the community. Find team-building strategies where people can connect while working on causes that have an impact on others' lives.

SITE VISIT: MANDEL PUBLIC LIBRARY OF WEST PALM BEACH

Background

The Mandel Public Library (in West Palm Beach, Florida) was brought to my attention by a strong recommendation from a library staff member. The staff member contacted me through e-mail to schedule a time to talk about her wonderful library. I happily agreed to meet with her the following week. During our initial meeting, she raved enthusiastically about her library and volunteered to arrange for me to tour the Mandel Public Library. What was so impressive about our meeting was that the staff member is a successful business owner, but she worked in the library part-time as a shelver because she loved the library. After the tour was arranged, I arrived at the Mandel Public Library and spent time with the director and the assistant library director. After talking to Chris (the director) and Lisa (the assistant director) for a few minutes, it became clear why the library staff member was so happy, committed, and engaged at work. What I noticed immediately is that Chris and Lisa have an easy dialogue with each other, along with feelings of mutual respect and affection, even though they are vastly different people. Chris is disarmingly charming and honest, with an endless number of laugh-out-loud stories sprinkled with a few wise anecdotes. Lisa is more of a planner, with a take-charge energy that gets things done. During the interview, Chris kept remarking that Lisa was the brains of the organization, and Lisa said that Chris was the glue that kept things running smoothly. They both were aware of each other's strengths and weaknesses, and they complemented each other perfectly.

Teamwork and Collaboration

After laughing and talking in the administrative office for a while, I made a note that Chris and Lisa have created a culture where the staff feel like they are part of a supportive family. They were even using the word "family" to describe the work culture. One of the things that both administrators stressed was the importance of hiring well in the beginning to avoid costly mistakes later. In some cases, they would redo the search more than once to find someone who fitted into the library's supportive work culture. When I asked them about "fit," the qualities they both agreed on were kindness, empathy, intellectual curiosity, creativity, and the ability to truly enjoy being in a diverse environment. Both of them said that you can always train the right candidate, but you cannot change inflexibility or a disdain for people. The two leaders believe strongly in flexibility. Because the library is open every day, the managers do not freak out or demand that staff members take sick or vacation time if they need to pick up their sick child or run a quick errand. Given this flexibility, the staff have responded by going out of their way to support each other during vacations or extended sick times. Chris and Lisa also allow the staff to explore new ideas without expecting things to be perfect. The result is more innovative programming where staff enjoy thinking outside the box. As we toured the library, they pointed with pride at the different staff-led projects, and I had to admit that the library looked fun, alive, and creative. The library has spaces for dance classes, art classes, an interactive teen center, and innovative studios and creative areas for music and other explorations. Even the signage was based on collaborative design thinking to increase customer engagement.

In terms of teamwork, the key was to respect each other's unique talents and figure out ways to work harmoniously together to bring projects to fruition. Teams naturally came together for the purpose of supporting the community in practical and creative ways. The staff kept saying that it was not about them but it was about the bigger goal, and as long as they kept the higher goal in view, they could resolve any differences that naturally occurred in the course of a special project. Another staffer said that because everyone helped and supported each other, it was easy to trust that the team members had your back, and this positively impacted accountability.

Although I had planned to spend only an hour at Mandel Library, I looked up and realized I had been there for over three hours and could easily have stayed for another hour. Once I left the building, the excited library staff member called me immediately to find out my impressions. I told her I'd had a lovely time, and she was already inviting me back because I had barely scratched the surface; they wanted to show me other impressive accomplishments and team collaborations. Now that is a glowing recommendation!

INTERVIEW WITH
Pamela Espinosa de los Monteros and Sandra Aya Enimil, Librarians

Pamela Espinosa de los Monteros is an assistant professor and the Latin American area studies librarian at Ohio State University (OSU). As a bilingual/bicultural information professional, she has supported international research initiatives, developed an award-winning educational curriculum, and served as a senior project manager in corporate, private, and higher education settings in the United States and Mexico. In her current role, Pamela liaisons with students, faculty, and staff of the Department of Spanish and Portuguese, the Diversity and Identity Studies Collective, the Latino/a Studies Program, and the Center for Latin American Studies.

At the time of my research, Sandra Aya Enimil, a licensed attorney, was the copyright services librarian and the head of Copyright Services at the OSU Libraries. (She is now the copyright librarian at Yale University.) At Ohio State, Sandra provided information and resources on using copyrighted materials and helped creators to protect their own copyrights. Sandra worked with many individuals and departments in the OSU Libraries (hereafter the Libraries) and across campus. She worked closely with colleagues in various academic units, Legal Affairs, and the Libraries' Special Collections and Digitization and Reformatting departments, to name a few.

The following interview focuses on the two librarians' approach to equity, diversity, and inclusion (EDI) training and their recruitment of participants. Their inclusive approach and efforts to bring in different and diverse team members resulted in better engagement, more advocates for EDI, and higher turnout for the trainings.

The Ohio State University Libraries was recommended to me for its potentially positive diversity initiatives. Many of the people who were excited about this library system attended the 2019 IDEAL conference, which took place on the Ohio State University campus. It was a pleasure talking with both ladies, and I look forward to visiting the campus soon.

Teamwork and EDI

Pamela and Sandra helped design and implement a pilot workshop model that promoted EDI to all interested workers in the Libraries through a series of self-assessments and group discussions. (EDI is the theme of the next chapter in this book. The profile here offers a positive counterpoint to the many challenges to diversity training, which I will address in the next chapter.)

Pamela and Sandra's use of teamwork was a big factor in the workshops' success. The EDI workshops were led by facilitators who were not the usual people of color coming together to create programs and policies. As co-chairs, Pamela and Sandra intentionally brought people of various backgrounds into the EDI workshop team to show how EDI is bigger than just diversity. Bringing a wider net to the EDI conversation literally "diversified" the initiative and brought different voices to a complex topic. Both ladies felt strongly about opening the discussion to a larger group, which resulted in wider participation in the workshops, and the inclusion of important topics like ageism, sexism, and working with people with disabilities in the EDI discussion.

How were you selected to co-chair the EDI pilot project? From what I was told, the committee stemmed from a larger commitment by the Ohio State University campus. Can you tell us a little more about the partnership?

We created the pilot together. Sandra was the co-chair of the University Libraries' Diversity and Inclusion Committee (now called the IDEAS Committee), and Pamela was a highly active member of that committee. The discussion to start this project came after we had a larger discussion about the Diversity and Inclusion Committee. The committee had been the recent recipient of a university award for its EDI work, but it had a hard time retaining an active membership. Active members felt burnt out and felt the work of the committee was professionally undervalued and fell disproportionately on minority faculty, staff, and a few allies. In addition, the Libraries' leadership had been discussing EDI values and an agenda that would more actively accord with the larger library and information science (LIS) community, but there was limited room for input, discussion, thought diversity, or nuance. The values expressed were noble, but they felt out of step with the existing EDI gaps that the organizational members navigated and were limited by on a daily basis.

The committee had not been subject to a review of committees that took place over two years, and it was determined that it should have been. During a meeting with the Libraries' Executive Committee and the Diversity and Inclusion Committee, members brought up their concerns regarding the committee's composition, purpose, and future direction. After this meeting, I asked Pamela if she would be willing to present a summary of our discussion at a meeting of the Libraries' Management Committee. She put together an amazing presentation and workshop that really highlighted what the committee had been wrestling with. The presentation would become the basis of the EDI@OSUL initiative. I then asked Pamela if she would be willing to partner with me to present an EDI workshop to everyone who might be interested in the entire library. We then approached the dean of the Libraries, Damon Jaggars, and let him know our idea and what we thought we needed to move forward. We asked for resources in the form of faculty/staff participation as facilitators and participants. We also asked for a representative from the Executive Team and for administrative support. We had support and authorization from the Libraries' Executive and Management committees to proceed.

When did you decide to open up and expand the EDI team beyond the traditional "all people of color" task force? What was your process for selecting people, and did anyone turn you down when you approached them to join?

The EDI@OSUL initiative intentionally moved away from traditional EDI approaches in the library. Before the initiative, much of the EDI work at the

University Libraries had been facilitated by external consultants, internal library advocates who are minorities, allies of underrepresented communities, or members of the Diversity and Inclusion Committee. The EDI work in these traditional EDI spaces was disproportionately distributed and was completed on a volunteer basis in addition to core professional duties, so the burden of EDI work was often placed on minority members of the library workforce and their allies.

As co-leaders of the initiative, we saw the limitations of this approach and wanted to pursue EDI as a collective effort to relieve the dependence of EDI work on the Libraries' internal minority and on the Diversity and Inclusion Committee's leadership.

Aside from attempting to resolve the work capacity issue, the initiative aimed to increase the number of resources that are required to bridge EDI gaps in a large organization. The work of a few, however strong and effective, is not enough to sustainably implement systemic change. In order for EDI to advance and be sustainable, EDI efforts, like anything else, are dependent on people and resources to make the change. To support this end, the initiative reframed EDI work as the work of the entire library organization. Therefore, we set out to recruit a diverse team for the initiative. The team consisted of staff from different backgrounds (e.g., individuals from majority groups as well as people of color), career levels (e.g., staff and faculty, managers, early-career, tenured/untenured), and library units (e.g., IT, HR, Public Services, Technical Services) who had varying levels of experience and expertise in facilitating conversations about EDI. The diversity of the resulting group was perhaps the initiative's most valuable asset. We wanted our library's workers to see themselves in the facilitators, as well as to realize that EDI work can be advanced for all. EDI work is not the work of Black and Brown people; regardless of our identity and background, we all have something to contribute to this space and to learn.

Some team members we identified, and others sought us out. We did not get turned down, which was a surprise given the fact that some people who volunteered already had a tremendous workload. The open disposition, cultural humility, and genuine interest of the group was contagious.

What are some key findings that you discovered from the workshop trainings? What surprised you the most during the workshop sessions?

We discovered that many library staff members struggle to articulate EDI solutions and actions. It is difficult to move EDI conversations from individuals espousing values and debating ideology or gaps to developing implementable ideas that will advance EDI in an organization. Some participants felt they lacked the language or training to inform or contribute to these solutions, others seemed weary of engaging in EDI because of their non-minority identity, and still others grappled with understanding what EDI is. Everyone was approaching EDI from a different level of competence and familiarity.

At the beginning the workshops felt tense. The audience anticipated and braced themselves for a lecture instead of a dialogue. To avoid this, we were careful to set a tone of openness, non-judgment, and community. The vulnerability of our facilitators—who disclosed their own EDI challenges and even their faux pas—helped the participants to open up and creatively explore EDI themes and topics. For some participants, it felt like the first time they had engaged in these discussions openly. Some groups had a hard time generating ideas and differentiating what were EDI gaps from general organizational gaps or challenges. Conveying their own values and criticizing what was not working in EDI proved easier for the participants to discuss than generating solutions, especially solutions that directly involved them. We also saw that the initial responses were just a generic list of EDI narratives that were commonly discussed in the LIS community. Participants seemed familiar with these narratives but were less familiar with how they could (or already did) engage, advocate, or work on their solutions.

The workshops reinforced the idea that EDI is a contact sport. This work requires vulnerability, intimacy, contact, awkwardness, and also occasional hits. Mobilizing individuals to learn about and advocate EDI is ultimately about organizational learning and leadership. If there are leadership gaps in the organization, they may be more likely to manifest as EDI disparities. There are also few spaces to openly discuss how an organization's members perceive and interpret EDI values and agendas in the library profession. It is important to make the time and space for the organization's members to reflect, discuss, and build a common understanding about what EDI values are and how members' work contributes to those values. The workshop helped to provide a starting point to gauge where our library's members were at, as well as what were areas of concern and interest.

If another organization wanted to implement your model at their institution, what would be your recommendations on how to get started?

We would be thrilled to share our model with other institutions. We recommend that other institutions wishing to get started should recruit a diverse team of colleagues who represent different aspects of the organization and who have a reputation for goodwill throughout the organization.

Tasking all library staff with the opportunity to think about and work through EDI challenges and opportunities provides a chance to tap into the problem-solving skills that librarians already have. When discussing EDI gaps, we recommend asking the participants to focus on ways that the average LIS employee can address systemic barriers to EDI in the organization.

Other institutions should push participants to recognize that embodying EDI values is not the same as adopting them as an ideology. The EDI@OSUL initiative attempted to reframe EDI work as actions informed by values. We should challenge participants to approach EDI methods and practices as things that emerge from iterative practice and are best designed within diverse groups. We should discourage virtue signaling or the perception that cultural competency is inherent or lacking from any specific identity group. We should encourage participants to understand that EDI work takes continued and dedicated practice, training, and education.

The success of EDI initiatives is dependent on institutional support and resources. Our initiative at the OSU Libraries would not have been possible without executive, middle management, and administrative support. ■ ■ ■

REFERENCES

Covey, Stephen. 2013. *The 7 Habits of Highly Effective People: Anniversary Edition*. Simon and Schuster.

Forbes. 2016. "13 Characteristics of a High-Performing Team." October 14. Forbes Coaches Council. www.forbes.com/sites/forbescoachescouncil/2016/10/14/13 -characteristics-of-a-high-performing-team-and-how-leaders-can-foster-them.

Lencioni, Patrick M. 2011. *The Five Dysfunctions of a Team: A Leadership Fable*. Jossey-Bass.

Maxwell, John. 2007. *21 Irrefutable Laws of Leadership: 10th Anniversary Edition*. HarperCollins.

Diversity, Equity, and Inclusion

have a confession to make. Before researching and writing this book, I had placed diversity, equity, and inclusion (DEI) initiatives on an island as they tried desperately to make a difference on the organizational mainland far away. Surrounding this DEI island was a sea of training, proven facts, book talks, diversity plans, diversity surveys and audits, recruitment plans, antiracist training, and cultural competencies. Today, DEI consulting, like management consulting, is a multibillion-dollar industry. However, as I was conducting my research for this book and asked companies, libraries, museums, and cultural heritage organizations about their long-term success stories and tangible results with regard to DEI, I could literally hear a pin drop. So, after hitting a brick wall for months, I finally talked to someone who gave me some simple advice. A wonderful Puerto Rican woman who works at Salesforce, and who absolutely loves her job, said that she was having no problem recruiting a diverse workforce. She enjoyed her job because her organization had worked on its workplace culture first, and with this strong foundation, they had been able to start to make progress on their DEI initiatives. She said the reason why most people are hitting a brick wall is because they see DEI as separate from workplace culture, when it is the positive result of a strong foundation and a healthy workplace culture. DEI cannot thrive without doing the hard work of changing the foundational structure of an organization. With this in place, the other DEI-related tools and resources have a real chance of making a difference. My informant was correct, and this knowledge turned my book around. I originally had DEI as my first chapter, but it is now the last chapter, as it is the final frontier in improving worker engagement. Once I started seeing DEI from this perspective, I found many diversity and inclusion success stories for this book.

DEI IN LIBRARIES

According to the American Library Association, 86 percent of its members identify as white, 81 percent identify as female, and the largest percentage of the workforce is in the 55–64 age group. With regard to academic and research libraries, the report "Inclusion, Diversity and Equity: Members of the Association of Research Libraries," published by Ithaka S+R, states that more than 75 percent of the employees at Association of Research Libraries (ARL) member institutions identified themselves as white. The report goes on to say that 89 percent of the librarians in leadership or administrative roles were white and non-Hispanic (McKenzie 2017).

The library profession, like other professions, has spent millions of dollars on inclusive recruitment, training, and consulting, but in the past thirty years, the profession's overall diversity numbers have remained static and, in some cases, have gotten worse.

Let Me Tell You a Story: Leaving the Library Profession

When I first started my research on diversity and inclusion with a focus on the library profession, there were lots of studies on recruitment strategies but not many on retention. This was shocking to me because I used to work at the Institute of Museum and Library Services (IMLS) at a time when we were giving out millions to recruit a diverse workforce. So, what happened? To answer this question, I put out a call on several discussions lists to see if I could locate people of color who had left the profession. After talking to a few people off the record, a few mentioned low pay and limited promotional opportunities, but most left because they felt excluded, ignored, and targeted at work. Many said that the isolation and exclusion affected their workplace self-esteem, so they decided to take their degree and reinvent themselves in a whole new profession.

The following story is from a person who left "library land" as he affectionately called the profession. It is a rather long story, but I selected this one because he was a former American Library Association Spectrum Scholar and requested his story be added in the book. Currently, he is excelling in a new career providing technology training, workshops, and consulting to underserved communities. This is his story:

. . . .

I was never interested in becoming a librarian, which is the ironic part of the story. My undergraduate degree is in computer science, and I was working as a computer programmer. It was my local librarian who kept telling me that the library profession could use someone with my technical expertise and there were plenty of high-paying jobs. She also said I would not go into debt because there were plenty of minority scholarships that would pay for my education because the library profession was begging for more diversity. My local librarian went a step further and e-mailed me some scholarship options and urged me to contact the American Library Association's Office of Diversity. To make a long story short, I applied and was accepted to the Spectrum Scholarship Program. Being a Spectrum Scholar was an amazing opportunity to meet new friends and network with people nationwide. What I did not anticipate was how difficult it would be to find my first job after graduation. After numerous rejections and months of frustration, I finally received a job offer as a librarian hundreds of miles away from my home in Philadelphia. As an African American male, I was a little nervous heading to the Midwest, but I knew I needed to remain flexible to get my new academic library career off the ground. Once I was hired, I noticed that I was the only African American male librarian out of twenty-three librarians, and amazingly, there were not many students or other people studying, group-studying, or researching in the library. When I inquired about the practically empty building, I was told that students did not like the library and preferred to study off campus. This seemed odd to me because most academic libraries are filled with students studying throughout the day, so I started to make inquiries with the student centers and faculty on campus. It was these discussions where I received quite a different perception about the library. The consensus was that the library was not a welcoming place for students or faculty, and everyone was strongly encouraged to conduct their research online or in group study at other campus locations. Determined to turn this around, I took the initiative to develop some fun technology-based programs that were designed to engage more students and bring more people into the library. Creating technology programs felt natural to me because of my computer science background. Because I spent most of my day at the reference desk, I promoted my reference hours, and eventually students and faculty would stop by during my reference shifts. Unfortunately, what I thought were strong outreach initiatives were met with anger and resistance. Once it became apparent that my outreach efforts were working, my supervisor, who until this point had pretended I did not exist, blindsided me with a disciplinary meeting. The meeting was with the head of Human Resources to officially tell me that my outreach efforts were a sign of insubordination and were against library policies and procedures. When I replied that I was not aware of these policies and procedures, I was told that they were in the documents I'd signed on the first day at the job. This whole process made me both mad and disheartened, so I made an appointment to talk with the library director. She told me that my direct supervisor was resistant to change and tended to react aggressively when the status quo was challenged. The director's solution was for me to try and meet with my supervisor more often and repair the broken relationship.

Unfortunately, my supervisor did not want to meet with me and declined my weekly meeting requests, and I was told to communicate everything in writing. I also started to notice other librarians distancing themselves from me, so out of frustration, I asked the only other person of color in the library out to lunch. During lunch, she told me that everyone was talking about how I was a little too excited about my new ideas and was ultimately asking for trouble. The librarians also resented my special professional development privileges because I had received outside minority-based scholarship funds to attend conferences and workshops. The library had been severely underfunded for years, so most of the librarians could not afford to attend national conferences. My friend informed me that the library's main focus is to provide online resources, and students and faculty should only come into the library if they need to check out resources or study quietly without making a sound. She confirmed that this was why the furniture and resources were old and outdated; it was because the campus is moving to more collaborative team-based learning, and new money is going into departments that embraced the strategic direction. She finally tried to reassure me by telling me to not take anything personally, that there was a revolving door for anyone who had "different" ideas from the status quo of maintaining a quiet, peaceful library at all times.

Confused by this long-term strategy, I went to the library director to talk about why the library was not creating a welcoming environment for students and faculty. The library director admitted that they needed to change, but the department managers strongly resisted the idea and insisted the library should always be a quiet place to study. She said that no one complained about the lack of funding, and the library provided valuable online resources to support the campus. After this disappointing meeting, I started to look for technology-based librarian jobs, but even with my computer science degree, I could not get past the phone interview. After a few months of this unsuccessful searching, I felt it deeply ironic that the profession that was begging for minority librarians was making it so hard for an African American man to get an academic job. Finally, I turned my attention outside the profession and, surprisingly, my combination of teaching, research, and computer science was attractive to many organizations. In no time, I found a dream job back in the Northeast working for a company committed to outreach and truly serving all communities. I am quite sure the statistics will say that I left for a higher-paying job, but in reality, I never felt welcomed in the library profession, and I felt more like a statistic than a human being. Now I realize that there are so many other options available that don't involve being disrespected for low pay and no recognition.

DYSFUNCTION AND LEAVING LIBRARY LAND

At first glance upon reading this man's story, it looks like that library could benefit from DEI training and antiracist work. And you would be correct; there are so many things wrong with this story, and especially the lack of true inclusion that pushed a talented person out the door. Yet, if we look at it through the lens of creating healthy work spaces, we can begin to unpack the overall dysfunction and the weak foundation that made it impossible for this organization to benefit from true diversity and inclusion. Let us look at just a few of the problems that we can identify from this story.

1. *Management resistant to change*—The direct supervisor was exhibiting a passive-aggressive management style that was resistant to new ideas. What is important to note is that the library director was aware of the supervisor's management style, but did not address the problem. The narrator of the story appears not to have been the first person who left because of this resistance, and everyone seemed to regard this as normal.

2. *Extinction followed by punishment*—The supervisor initially paid no attention to the employee (pretending he did not exist) and then wrote him up (punishment) instead of providing him with continual and timely feedback (performance management). Once a written reprimand was issued, the supervisor went back to ignoring the employee and forced him to put things in writing, which is still a passive-aggressive form of punishment.

3. *Lack of recognition and praise*—Even if the librarian was going against policies and procedures that he might not be aware of, he should still have been praised for taking some initiative and wanting to positively support the organization. His heart was in the right place, and this should have been the time for flexibility, adaptability, and continual communication, not punishment and isolation.

4. *Performance evaluation/feedback*—There was a definite breakdown in communication in terms of supervisor-employee relations. The employee should never have to be the one taking the lead in repairing the relationship. The employee should not have to beg the supervisor for a meeting or put all his thoughts in writing. Instead, the supervisor should be meeting with the employee regularly and talking about goals, aspirations, and objectives. If this had happened from the start, the supervisor would have known about the employee's outreach plans and communicated why they would or would not work for the organization.

5. *Keeper of the status quo*—What is especially notable—and disturbing—in the narrator's story is that the library is not in alignment with the campus. The students and faculty members know they are not welcome in the library. As a result, the campus administration has not increased the library's budget, and the library suffers from limited resources (old furniture and limited professional development funds) because it is not committed to creating an inclusive, welcoming environment for its major stakeholders. The library administration knows that they are not receiving crucial resources because of this work political stance but are unwilling to change. As a new employee, the narrator had no idea what lengths the library would go to keep the status quo until he tried to change the environment.

You might say that the supervisor is just being that way to the African American male employee because of implicit bias, microaggressions, or racist behaviors. That is a true statement, but it tells only part of the story. Remember, the work colleague said that other librarians had left because new ideas were met with cold resistance and isolation. When the library director allows the supervisor to treat her employees with contempt for challenging the status quo and then they walk out the door, that is a weak foundation that will prevent any DEI initiatives from thriving, even with diversity training, workshops, and performance metrics. What I find is that grappling with these toxic issues of the broader workplace culture is where the hard work truly begins, and this is what most organizations are not willing to address because change takes work and affects everyone, not just marginalized populations.

In terms of the organization, when the employee used his unique talents (technology, campus engagement, and people skills) to bring new customers into the library, he was not only punished but was left feeling isolated and alone. I would wager that the library initially thought they were doing the right thing by diversifying the workforce and picking an African American male to join the faculty. Yet they saw him as a mere number, a statistic, and viewed his hiring as "the right thing to do" without understanding the true benefits of diversity. Diversity is not beneficial until the organization truly embraces the uniquely valuable skills, talents, and abilities of the person being recruited. Not only did our narrator take the initiative and reach out to the library's stakeholders, but he also quickly identified a strategy to make campus faculty, students, and staff feel included. And when he left, not only did the library lose an African American male hire (which is discouraging), but a person who could have elevated the image of the library. The library may well hire a replacement who goes along with the status quo, but eventually disengagement will set in because the organization is not committed to a healthy workplace culture.

DEI TRAINING IS ABSOLUTELY NECESSARY BUT WILL NEVER WORK WITHOUT CHANGING THE CULTURE

I can hear many of the people I interviewed for this book saying: "Hey, what about diversity training? Doesn't that help?" First, let me go on the record to say that I believe that DEI training is necessary to create awareness and provide an ongoing framework for discussion and critical conversations. Racism in the library profession does exist. People are human, not perfect, and will make mistakes, so having the right tools to support a more inclusive, supportive, diverse environment is absolutely needed. However, diversity, equity, and inclusion training does not work on its own because in many cases we are ignoring the dysfunctional work environments, which is the foundation that sets the tone for real change. And I always say, it is easier to schedule a diversity training than it is to tackle bad leadership, toxic teams, and persistent low morale and distrust. These are all hard issues, but ignoring the workplace culture does not benefit the organization and can potentially result in a hostile work environment.

Diversity Training Does Not Work

Social psychologists have many theories to explain why diversity training does not work as intended. Studies show that diversity training generates backlash and that mandatory diversity training has resulted in more hostility in the workplace. Researchers also see evidence of "irresistible stereotypes," or biases so deeply ingrained that they simply cannot be taught away in a one-day workshop (Cullen 2007). Pamela Newkirk reported on a study that showed large expenditures on diversity have also failed (Newkirk 2019).

Dobbin and Kalev, both sociologists, examined three decades of data from more than 800 U.S. firms and interviewed hundreds of managers and executives. The study took an especially dim view of mandatory diversity training, which was found to trigger a backlash against those it was intended to help.

Universities have responded by pledging hundreds of millions of dollars to increase faculty diversity, including a $50 million commitment by Yale, nearly $23 million by Dartmouth, $25 million by Johns Hopkins, $60 million by Cornell, and $165 million by Brown. . . . While these initiatives have helped power the multibillion-dollar diversity training industry, there is little indication that they have resulted in more diversity or less bias. And there is some evidence that some of the anti-bias strategies can actually make matters worse (Newkirk 2019).

DEI and Emotions: Yes, Emotions!

One of my favorite workshops to give is my talk on persuasion research and influence. During my undergraduate education, my favorite classes were social psychology, market research, and persuasion. Persuasion is my favorite subject to research, and the basic theories have remained true in almost all areas of my work. The one statement that is 100 percent true is that people make decisions based on their emotions and then justify it with logic and reasoning (i.e., their intellect). Before the advent of social media, this was true at least 80 percent of the time, but experts say it may be closer to 95 percent today. This is hard to accept because people hate hearing that they can be influenced or maybe manipulated. At this point in the workshop, I casually mention that politics, religion, and race are such emotionally charged topics that people have killed or been killed because of their emotional attachment to a belief. Emotions are hard to change, and logic and intellect make little difference until some other emotional incident occurs to alter the person's perspective. For instance, police brutality and people fighting for change have been going on for years with plenty of facts, statistics, and evidence, but it was not until people witnessed the George Floyd murder on their TV sets that the conversation began to change. How does this impact diversity, equity, and inclusion? As someone who studies emotions and persuasion, I always cringe a little when organizations ask me for the right DEI survey, checklist, plan, or statistics when it comes to DEI work. These tools do not tap into the emotions surrounding race, privilege power, the status quo, and the intense resistance to change and grow as an organization. Like the example at the beginning of the chapter, from my interviews with libraries all over the world, there are plenty of examples of libraries who are not receiving necessary resources because they refuse to adapt and change or align with the campus strategic direction. Others argue with me that they are tapping into emotions when they try to get the dominant culture to own up to racism, privilege, and oppression as a means to change behavior. However, as I mentioned in earlier chapters, negative reinforcement does not change long-term behavior; only positive reinforcement can do this effectively. Let's take a look at another plan to not only address DEI but also the elephant in the room, toxic workplace culture.

A HEALTHY WORKPLACE BLUEPRINT: BEYOND DIVERSITY STATEMENTS AND DIVERSITY PLANS

Strengthening the foundation of the workplace culture is a better way to strengthen an organization's commitment to DEI initiatives. This is not easy work, and in some cases, it will require making hard decisions in terms of management, performance expectations, recognition, and embracing diverse ideas and perspectives. Trust me, it is easier to have people of color write diversity statements, create diversity plans, and talk about antiracism than it is to make decisions that will make others uncomfortable. Although in most cases it is bad for morale and inclusion, the status quo feels like a worn but comfortable pair of shoes that you don't want to take off under any circumstances. Yet an organization will not benefit from DEI until it is not only open to diverse perspectives but truly understands that by embracing new voices, the organization's culture itself will change for the better. The organization will continue to have problems until the workplace understands that DEI is a crucial part of a transformational culture rather than just a stat, a check-off list, or a recruitment plan.

So, what is a healthy workplace blueprint? Is it another strategic plan? No, because for the most part, the strategic plan looks at external customers and the external environment. The healthy workplace blueprint looks at the internal environment; that is, how people feel (emotions) about working at their institution. The goal should move from the status quo and complacency to engagement, inclusion, and ultimately transformative change. This blueprint needs to involve *everyone* and provide a framework for the future.

This is not a quick destination but a journey where the organization continues to evolve and get better. The first question before any blueprint is started is to have the hard conversation about why we are working toward a more diverse, equitable, and inclusive culture. This may seem obvious, but you would be surprised that everyone in your organization is not on the same page. From my consultant work, I find that there is a good deal of assumptions about DEI, such as that everyone is on the same page and we are all moving in one direction. But by starting with the "why," you will find various answers from "doing the right thing" to "pressure from our organization" and "racial politics at work" to giving people jobs that they may/may not deserve. This is a very hard conversation, but it's a crucial step to tackle the messaging head-on in the beginning. Working toward a diverse, equitable, and inclusive environment is the final frontier, the type of environment that reflects back to a strong workplace culture and nurturing, supportive climate that elevates all employees. If this is not consistently reinforced and misconceptions based on fear, stereotypes, and short-term thinking are not tackled, future initiatives are bound to fail. With this blueprint, it is easier to develop a leadership vision that directly aligns with the organization's overall goals. It is important to note that the blueprint should make people feel great and provide a positive outlook for the future. It is crucial to tap into emotions and feelings because it is emotions that will propel people to long-term action. This is similar to the leadership's vision, but it is different because it focuses on the whole organization and how everyone needs to participate to see results.

Some questions to ask include: What would it feel like to be appreciated for your individual talents and strengths in the organization? What needs to be done to get from the current situational analysis to a healthier work culture? What do we expect leadership to do to make sure everyone feels valued in the organization? Can we improve how we recognize and praise all employees? Can we strengthen our feedback and evaluation loops? How do we work together and get things done, and can this process be improved? Are we engaging in positive reinforcement or in penalty, punishment, and negative reinforcement in terms of our policies? How can we go from the status quo to embracing a future that challenges us but will benefit everyone on the other side? What is our stance on new ideas, making mistakes, and embracing change? How can we strengthen trust? From there we can think about all the benefits of not only recruiting diverse people but also how this benefits the organization, the customers, and the profession.

Healthy Organizational Climate and DEI Barriers: The Hard Work

After the healthy workplace blueprint has been created, the next step is where the hard work begins for the organization. I would love to say that positive emotions and good feelings will carry the organization to the victory line, but the status quo is always present and a powerful deterrent. There are specific reasons why a workplace culture has low engagement and low morale. There is a reason why some people love their job and others are being bullied and harassed in the same organization. There is a reason why people are counting down to their retirement or the next vacation. There is a reason why the organization keeps creating DEI surveys, plans, and statements without any results. This is where the organization needs to be real and write down the barriers to creating a healthy organization. This is scary and requires trust without penalty and punishment. You can only change what you can see. Once you have this list, then you can draw up targeted plans on how to remove barriers in the organization. This doesn't involve a "one size fits all" training or workshop, but a plan of action that is tailored to your specific organization. If this is difficult, I suggest hiring an organizational development/DEI consultant you can trust for an unbiased assessment. But however you do it, a targeted plan of action is a crucial step that is needed to move from good feelings to action and real results.

DEI Work Revisited: Who Should Be in the Room

Note that I've changed the phrase "DEI work" to a "healthy workplace blueprint," which redistributes the responsibility solely from marginalized employees and staff onto everyone working together to make lasting change. Instead of forcing diverse people to figure out complex organizational development issues disguised as a DEI plan, it is time for the organization to figure out who needs to be at the table to move the agenda forward. Amanda

Fernandez, the founder of Inclusifyy, said it best: an organization needs three categories of people when it comes to this work—power, expertise, and lived experiences. "Power," of course, means someone who makes decisions to move the ideas and plans forward. "Expertise" means someone who understands organizational development, DEI work, and facilitation. "Lived experiences" can mean people of color, professional staff, and other people who are passionate and committed to making lives better at work. Let us be clear: even when an organization develops a stronger foundation for a healthy workplace culture, diversity, equity, and inclusion training and awareness are still needed. They have just been taken off the island and now have a major seat at the table, where they belong.

DEI: THE FINAL FRONTIER

I have a story from my work that lines up with my theory. I didn't see it when I started this book because I kept thinking of DEI as the dominant (white) culture accepting diverse voices and perspectives. Once I changed my theory to how DEI can transform a work environment, I recalled a unique personal story that will tie everything together.

When I first arrived as the executive director of the African-American Research Library and Cultural Center (AARLCC), there was an employee who had been placed in our building after being rejected at multiple locations. Interesting enough, Steve is white, and he was close to retirement age. His former boss informed me that he was set in his ways with "declining skills," so they had dropped him off at our library. Steve's ego was hurt, so naturally it took him some time to get over the rejection. However, Steve was friendly, upbeat, and a hard worker, and after some observation, we noticed he had some underutilized talents. Steve was an amazing writer, so we gave him the assignment of writing the library press releases, at which he excelled. He also played guitar and experimented with video and video-editing as a hobby, so we challenged him to create fun projects that promoted the library. Most of the videos he made were light-hearted and designed to make you smile (in a good way), and we found that the customers loved the creativity. As we continued to recognize and praise Steve for trying new things, he really blossomed, and his positive energy, engaging press releases, and fun videos were recognized across Broward County. Within a few years, the AARLCC went from being pitied to being showcased in the news and winning numerous awards for creativity and innovation. Steve went from our photographer to our videographer, graphic designer, press release expert, tour guide, media expert, and holiday "let's get this party started" organizer. Predictably, Steve's efforts were favorably noticed by his old work colleagues, and like the classic song "I Will Survive," the old lovers came from outer space wanting him back. After four years, these lovers were quick to point out that an old white guy did not fit at the African-American Research Library and Cultural Center, and his talents were better suited for a larger level. I told Steve he could go, but we cared for him and he was an important part of the team. Steve, now feeling a new lease on life, wrote a heartwarming letter to his old work colleagues telling them that he loved working at the AARLCC and would stay put there until his retirement. He did retire a few years later, with a huge send-off from our staff and the community members who loved him.

At the time, we had no idea about employee engagement trends, motivation, positive or negative reinforcement, and so on. We just noticed Steve's talents and created an environment where he could be the best version of himself. And by so doing, our organization benefited from his expertise, which helped us win awards and national recognition.

If we had just ignored Steve and allowed him to be a photographer or forced him to do something else that didn't bring out the best version of himself, our organization would not have benefited from his diverse talents. This is why DEI is the last chapter of this book. By doing the inner work and getting the other things right in your organization, you will be better equipped to benefit from the diverse perspectives and amazing talents that are currently in your organization. You will also have a stronger foundation with which to retain top talent and create a network where people want to work at your organization—and move beyond the paycheck and benefits to greater belonging, healthier self-esteem, and, like Steve, self-actualization that is truly gratifying.

DIVERSITY, EQUITY, AND INCLUSION: RECOMMENDATIONS

- Take DEI off the island and develop strategies to improve the overall health of the organization. If everyone is miserable or underperforming, then how do you expect diverse people to come in and thrive? Create a stronger foundation that benefits everyone at all levels of the organization.

- For the healthy workplace blueprint, everyone needs to participate and provide input. This is not something for minority employees to handle by themselves while everyone else lives an alternative existence. Positive workplace culture impacts everyone.
- If what is holding you back from transforming the environment are policies and procedures, revisit them and change, eliminate, and revise them as necessary. If any policies create oppression and preserve the status quo, those policies should be challenged and revised.
- The organization must believe in intentionally creating a diverse and inclusive work culture. As noted in the stories about the Richland County and Hillsboro County libraries (see below), the vast majority of library school graduates are white women, so we need to take a close look at our hiring practices if we want to build teams that truly reflect the diversity of our community—as these libraries did.
- True diversity and inclusion will be challenging because changing the workplace culture will not miraculously turn around; some tough decisions will probably need to be made for the organization to create a more engaged environment.
- The actual recruitment of employees is not where you get the benefits of a diverse workforce; the actual benefits are from engaged and productive employees who are using their natural talents to benefit the organization.
- After DEI training workshops, make sure there is a built-in strategy for positive reinforcement, peer recognition, and praise for moving in the right direction. Don't depend on just the workshops and training to change behavior. Inaction is still negative reinforcement. Make sure the organization is "reinforcing" behavior that it wants to change the culture.

SUCCESS STORIES

This section offers three success stories from libraries that have made significant headway in terms of employee engagement and recruiting and retaining diverse talent. Are the following libraries perfect models that should be the standard for all libraries? The answer is no. This work takes time, and as I stated in the introduction, it will not be an overnight fix. It will take a new mindset to elevate your library and ultimately benefit from engaged, productive, and happier employees.

Richland County Library's Leadership Team and Staff

Melanie Huggins is executive director of the Richland County Library (the library system of Columbus, South Carolina). Prior to this, she was executive director of the St. Paul Public Library in Minnesota. In 2012 the South Carolina Library Association named her Librarian of the Year. Focused on the future of libraries, Melanie has also served on the IMLS National Task Force to Define 21st Century Skills for Museums and Public Libraries, and in 2015 was recognized internationally by Denmark's Dokk1 on their Wall of Inspiration.

When I first started seeking recommendations for success stories, the Richland County Library kept coming up as a complete model for employee engagement. I could tell after talking to Melanie and reviewing the library's materials that all the praise and glowing recommendations were well deserved. I also had the privilege of talking with several library staff members ranging from branch managers, to children's librarians, to the security guards. The responses to my questions (below) are the results of a group process. Everyone was friendly and welcoming and enjoyed answering my questions. The county library's management encourages staff to try new things, such as playtime to explore new technologies, and professional development days for team-building and bonding. The Richland County Library is also committed to recruiting and retaining a diverse and talented workforce. The library has made special efforts to recruit people of color to more senior positions, and as a result, more than 40 percent of its branch managers are now from diverse backgrounds.

How does your leadership team build trust and engagement with your employees?

Richland Library leaders are invested in building trust throughout our organization. We hold quarterly retreats with managers from across the system to communicate updates, share priorities, and address any issues or concerns that we have heard from staff. Managers are empowered to communicate with transparency so all staff can share in moving our vision forward.

Trust is built when the staff at all levels can inform decision-making. The development of our strategic plan is a good example of collaborative decision-making across organizational levels. A cross-functional "Strategic Plan Refresh Team" was charged with learning about community needs and evaluating library priorities. Then, the staff in every department and location participated in human-centered design workshops to think about ways they could contribute to our strategic plan's goals. This level of engagement builds trust and buy-in from all staff.

In an effort to stay connected, staff from each of our library locations can sit down and share information with our library's internal and external communication coordinators. They can provide insight into customer experiences, community partnerships, staff accolades, top resources, and any questions or concerns that customers or staff may have.

What programs have you implemented to support your branch managers?

Location managers need unique support because they are critical to our library's success, and they are often working with constraints like time, capacity, and distance from our main location. We have recently implemented two programs that serve all managers, and they are especially helpful to our location managers.

Our Supervisor Learning Circles use the P2PU methodology and focus on a curriculum developed by our Learning Engagement Department and team of talented staff. Managers throughout the system spend six weeks learning from and supporting each other in celebrating and sustaining our culture of outstanding customer service.

Our Becoming a Better Supervisor program, which launched in 2020, was created as a direct result of feedback from our managers and supervisors. Over the course of the year, all managers will have a chance to learn about the varied roles of a supervisor, increase confidence in dealing with policies and employee relations issues, and identify tools and resources that will help them continue to grow as leaders.

The Richland Library also supports location managers with opportunities through our Learning Engagement Department. They offer more than a half-dozen programs each month that shine a spotlight on different departments across the system. These programs cover budgetary training, highlight customer service improvements, promote leadership, and address diversity, equity, and inclusion.

What was your diversity recruitment strategy that resulted in 40 percent of your managers being people of color?

We believe in intentionally creating a diverse and inclusive work culture. With statistics indicating that most library school graduates are white women, we knew we would need to examine our hiring practices if we want to build teams that truly reflect the diversity of our community. By making the MLIS degree a preferred qualification rather than a requirement, we've been able to hire immensely talented professionals who have the experience and skills needed to be managers in our library system—even though they lack the formal degree.

Together, we are part of something larger. We are building a culture based on open, respectful conversations that allow us all to learn about one another as individuals, with different perspectives and life experiences.

What advice would you give to retain great employees?

Retention, like so much else, comes back to organizational culture. Our goal is for Richland Library staff to know they are making a difference in our community, and they have the tools, skills, resources, and decision-making authority to create exceptional experiences for our customers.

We are also able to offer a strong benefits package, growth and development opportunities, and the ability to explore an employee's passions through their work. Our talented staff offer amazing learning experiences for our customers—from fiber arts to virtual reality—because they can connect their personal interests to their work at the library. Then it translates into sharing these interests with the community.

Another unique benefit that we offer is "Project Play." Each week, staff are encouraged to devote thirty minutes to an hour of work time to playing. Some staff do puzzles. Others paint or draw. The idea is to take a break from the day-to-day and allow the mind to relax, which in turn promotes creativity. Ultimately, this helps staff feel happier and be more productive.

Could you walk us through the steps on how your staff can volunteer to help their favorite charity during work time?

Full-time employees, with supervisor approval, are eligible for up to one hour of release time weekly to volunteer. Employees can serve at any local 501(c)(3) organization, addressing a community need. They are responsible for contacting the organization they are interested in and completing the volunteer process—with their work schedule in mind. Then employees submit their service hours monthly to the volunteer coordinator and copy their supervisors. The volunteer coordinator is available to assist with any part of this process.

In keeping with the library's vision statement, the goal is to "enhance the quality of life for our entire community." Library administration wants to enhance the library's culture of caring and learning at a workplace where staff find personal meaning in their work while also feeling like they are making a difference in the community. The library supports this procedure because we believe it is an important tool in supporting a work-life balance. Employees are encouraged to volunteer with organizations in which they have a personal interest, and they are solving a local problem by making a difference in the community. ■ ■ ■

INTERVIEW WITH
Stephanie Chase and Hillary Ostlund

Stephanie Chase is the former director of the Hillsboro Public Library in Oregon. She has more than twenty years' experience in local and municipal government and has served communities ranging from small rural ones in New England, to resort communities, to some of our largest urban centers on both the East and West Coasts. Stephanie is an accomplished innovator and change leader, with significant experience leading organizational design and effectiveness and community engagement initiatives.

Hillary Ostlund is a manager at the Hillsboro Public Library. She currently leads the library's Cultivate team, which is focused on staff development, training, and employee engagement. A continuous learner with a background in design thinking, Hillary is always looking for ways to bring inspiration and ideas into the workplace while matching people's strengths to their work.

Stephanie and Hillary were recommended to me by three different library directors. After speaking with them for a half hour on a conference call, I knew I had found kindred spirits. At the time we talked, I was feeling frustrated after connecting with several recommended organizations only to hear workplace horror stories that would keep you up at night. Within minutes, we felt like old friends who were catching up after a long break. Upbeat and positive, both women are determined to make a difference. They are willing to take chances, admit mistakes, and challenge the status quo to create a more engaged, creative, and inclusive work environment.

Early in our conversation, Hillary and Stephanie made it clear that they did not have to make any major changes in their organization. The library already had amazing circulation numbers and vibrant programs and was known to be an integral part of the community. However, as leaders, they knew they could do better and, more importantly, attract a more diverse clientele into the library. Hillsboro is one of the most diverse communities in Oregon, and they wanted their staff to be a positive reflection of this and create a more seamless, customer-friendly experience. One of the first changes they made was to invest heavily in the professional development of the staff, using various strategies to support the growth and progress of staff members. The next step was to utilize design thinking principles to reconfigure library spaces and eventually eliminate all the information and reference desks. Once those desks had been removed, the organization instituted a form of roving reference called "orbiting." With regard to teamwork and collaboration, the library created new teams (a merchandising and display team, an innovation team, etc.) that matched the new direction of the library. And as for creativity and innovation, the library developed a culture of continuous evaluation where if they see something is wrong, they are willing to make changes even if they may not know whether the results will be perfect. Both managers admitted that they have tried things that didn't work, but this is all part of the creative process, and innovation comes when you are willing to make mistakes.

With regard to DEI, the Hillsboro Public Library has some impressive diversity recruitment numbers that were a result of changing the job descriptions. To ensure that the library reflects the diversity of the community, the management team took a closer look at the job descriptions and educational requirements and actively figured out how to attract and hire a diverse pool of candidates. They try to view the recruitment and retention process through a lens of what they can do to both add value to the library and support the community in all its diversity. In this philosophy, the organization is willing to ask tough questions and challenge stereotypes and biases as they progress in supporting a diverse workforce that has representation at all levels of the organization.

How did you get your library staff on board for change management? How did you keep your staff feeling engaged through a culture of constant change and experimentation?

Everyone always wants a "silver bullet" or "magic wand" for this, but the answer is to communicate, communicate, communicate. In any change process, you must recognize that not everyone will be happy, certainly at first, and you must be willing to give space and time for people to get on board.

We are very inspired by William Bridges' change and transition models, but we have really taken to focusing on our ambassadors and early adopter staff to help lead the changes. It is immensely powerful to have the discussion and support for a change led by the staff themselves, as opposed to being led purely by management.

We purposely use the term "evolution" instead of "change" to imply that this is part of the new way of workplaces and organizations that must adapt constantly to meet the community's needs and expectations. We are dedicated to strongly communicating this message, too, particularly as part of the hiring process. Our work serving our community will never be done because our community is rapidly growing and changing, too.

Tell us about the redesigned teams. Did the adjustments result in more customer reengagement?

We do have a redesigned structure in general (our quadrants) and staff-led teams, what we call "work circles," and project-level teams. So, we could answer this in several ways . . . and we weren't really working on this for a customer "reengagement" so much as to provide less siloed services, easier access for patrons, and to be nimbler in implementing changes to our services based on patron requests.

How does your library organization handle conflict?

We do not allow for triangulation (and we expect people to talk with each other). We encourage an atmosphere where people are encouraged to speak up. We provide opportunities for staff to share feedback: through surveys, Slack channels, informal chats or meetings with leadership, and one-on-one meetings with supervisors. We rely on resources we have available to us through our city government resources; this includes Human Resources and access to employee benefits and our Police Department, who have mediation training and safety resources available to us.

How did you change your job descriptions in order to attract a wider and more diverse workforce? What have been the results of your DEI efforts?

We use values-based recruitment and language in job descriptions, focusing on core values both in our city and within our library. We have made great efforts to increase diversity in all its aspects in our staffing, but we still have a long way to go. We want patrons to see themselves represented in our staff, and we want our staff to feel that sense of community and camaraderie with one another as well, particularly so that people of color do not feel alone. Even recently, after many years of this deliberative work, we recently had a staff member express how "white" our staff still feels, and that it is difficult to know how to engage and operate on committees or teams.

It has been clearly acknowledged that the profession of librarianship is exclusive. It is a profession made up mostly of white women; and many of us have been in positions, current or in the past, where we have been able to do this work because we have a partner who makes enough that we can afford to. A library degree is expensive, in most cases, and also doesn't guarantee you'll be able to easily obtain a position that compensates you for it. So much about this picture has to change, and all of us who are local hiring managers have the ability to address part of it; this starts with thinking, for each and every job, what is truly required for someone to be successful, as well as how much a new staff member truly needs to be able to know or do in their earliest days on the job. For us, with each open position, we ask ourselves what the key skills and necessary experience are, and we recruit for that—not for what has been in the past, but what is needed *now*. We also look at what's happening in the organization to see how much we can support learning in the moment; while some open positions do need someone to have the experience to jump in the deep end right away, many don't. Having an organization dedicated to continuous learning means we should look for opportunities for staff to be learning from day one instead of expecting a specific, fixed, high level of expertise from the get-go.

We must think about what experiences, education, and contributions can add to enhance our services in libraries. What if we are open to candidates with other backgrounds? Do we need college-level degrees for our positions? Let us talk about the MLIS degree and when it really makes sense. How do we encourage our community members to apply for jobs in libraries to help expand the reach of the library and continue to build trust with our communities? We will not know until we start to see these changes in our staffing models, and it starts with unpacking job descriptions and breaking down bureaucratic barriers, which we see too often in libraries and governmental structures.

What are some of your strategies to retain a diverse workforce?

We hope that the transition to our self-managed, horizontal structure will play a large part in this: by emphasizing the leadership roles staff at all levels can have, and the ability staff have to make decisions, implement changes, and give voice to their concerns, we are hearing from many more staff members. This results in many more voices and opinions at the table and really breaks down the idea that there is only "one right way" to do something; this speaks to being a truly collaborative environment.

This is not to say that we do not have guidelines, policies, or structure—we do. Through our Quality Service Standards and our Great Expectations, our organization has made its priorities clear, and the key is how each individual staff person implements or responds to those expectations can be very personal. In most organizations, what the employees are trying to do is cooperate, to do their best to carry out what someone else wants; the latter is typically the person or the group that is perceived as having the most power, and there is not a lot of opportunity to influence what the outcome truly is. Those with privilege in a collaborative work environment might describe it as messy; we do our best to instead celebrate the diversity of opinion, opportunities, options, and voices, and view these as the incredible gifts our staff are sharing with one another and with the organization as a whole.

How do you recognize and praise excellent work? Do you still celebrate wins even if the organization may be making a mistake?

We recognize staff by using our Slack channel for "bravos." We encourage celebrating daily work and achievements for all aspects of service. Our staff newsletters call out work anniversaries, and we include a comment for each staff member, in addition to recognizing achievements at our all-staff meetings and end-of-year celebration. We also have a "Shining Star" award for our city government resources, and we nominate staff when we see extra efforts made; several have won this award. We are also always aware of other awards and benchmarks, and we try to cultivate this type of awareness in our supervisors and staff when it comes to recognizing coworkers, colleagues, and staff members. This is especially important to us!

We think of mistakes differently than failure. We make mistakes each and every day and try extremely hard to learn from them and encourage talking through mistakes to see how we can improve together going forward. This perspective on mistakes is what we believe contributes to our having very few "failures." What has worked is celebrated, and that is what we focus on.

Tell us a little more about "orbiting." Has this new form of roving reference increased your engagement with customers who visit the library?

"Orbiting" is what our staff decided to call roving, or our holistic point-of-need service. Both traditional "reference" service and traditional "circulation" service are provided through this deskless service model.

One of the reasons we instituted orbiting was to allow our users to choose the level of engagement they want to have with our staff. We knew we had many patrons who did not want to interact with staff—they wanted to be able to come in and use the library on their own terms, and having to interact with staff likely *reduced* their satisfaction and engagement with the library. The rapid adoption of our self-service changes shows this to be true; more than 95 percent of our checkouts are now via self-check, and we have implemented self-service in room booking and fine payment with no negative customer comment.

This freed up time for our staff to engage with the customers who wanted to engage. In traditional library service models, especially at a library as busy as ours (we have nearly one million visits annually between our two locations), there's simply not the time to really deeply engage on a regular basis—there's someone else who needs help or there's a long line. Orbiting has really allowed us to engage with our customers who do want an engagement experience, and we hear about this on a daily basis through patrons' comments. Those comments have switched from mainly being about lines (or, unfortunately, negative interactions with staff) to praising our staff. We receive almost no negative feedback about our staff and our service (although a small number of users still ask for the desks to come back). ■ ■ ■

INTERVIEW WITH
Alyssa Jocson Porter and Lynn Kanne

Alyssa Jocson Porter is a tenured reference and instruction librarian at Seattle Central College, where she is the liaison to the STEM and Creative Arts programs and coordinates collection development. She coauthored the chapter "I, Too: Unmasking Emotional Labor of Women of Color Community College Librarians" in *Pushing the Margins: Women of Color Librarians in LIS* (2018) and recently wrote a blog post, "POC Librarians: Claiming Conferences Spaces," for WOC+Lib. She is Filipina American.

Lynn Kanne started at Seattle Central College in 1998 as a tenured library faculty member, and she coordinated reference services and liaised with faculty in science and math and culinary arts. Since 2015 she has served as dean for libraries, eLearning, and employee development. Lynn holds an MLIS degree from the University of Washington and a BA in American studies from the University of California at Santa Cruz.

I found Seattle Central College by mistake. A friend and colleague recommended that I read the book *Pushing the Margins: Women of Color Librarians in LIS*. Though she had pointed me to a specific book chapter, it was Alyssa and Lynne's "I, Too: Unmasking Emotional Labor of Women of Color Community College Librarians" that stood out for me. It mentioned that of the six librarians at their library (at Seattle Central College), three were women of color. I needed to know more about minority recruitment and retention and how they had achieved a 50 percent split for people of color. I initially talked to Alyssa Jocson Porter. She mentioned that the team tends to pull together when conflict arises, because they have spent time creating spaces where they can have difficult conversations. Cultural competency training has given the staff a framework for current and future conversations with new and potential employees. Alyssa encouraged me to talk to her library dean, Lynn Kanne. She complimented Lynn for providing a supportive environment that allows them to move forward as a team. Lynn in turn credited her library team for rolling up their sleeves and doing the difficult work. She stressed that Seattle Central College is committed to creating an environment where everyone feels included, welcome, and invited. The library wants to serve as a positive example of this ongoing work.

What advice would you suggest for organizations that are hiring new employees and making sure that they support DEI? What procedures do you have in place in terms of onboarding and initial training?

Alyssa: My advice would be to demonstrate that diversity and equity initiatives are in action, not just a statement. During the screening/interviewing process at our library at Seattle Central College, we make our commitment to diversity and equity known in several places: in the job description, in the supplemental questions of the application, and in the interview questions we ask. Also, if a prospective candidate were to look up our library's website, they would easily be able to find evidence of our library's diversity and social justice work (not just a statement but embedded evidence, e.g., examples of programming, resources, and curriculum). The reiteration of this theme should signal to applicants that diversity and equity matter to us, and that if they join our team, they can expect to contribute to this work.

For onboarding and initial training, I would suggest incorporating several aspects of diversity, such as reviewing preferred pronouns and accessibility accommodations. We should also outline our expectations, our training, and provide a process for review/feedback.

For our library's Reference Assistant (RA) program, we have developed a Canvas training module for our new RAs, which includes basic information about reference work but also readings about critical pedagogy and librarianship. This gives the RAs an opportunity to reflect on and discuss the systems and structures within our field.

How does your organization handle conflict and tension between employees? What strategies does the staff use to strengthen teamwork and collaboration throughout the year?

Alyssa: I am struggling with this question about handling tension among employees. I am aware that what might be a healthy work environment for one person might be a toxic work environment for someone else. Our library has multiple ways of addressing conflict: communication among ourselves, mediation through the dean, and Human Resources if necessary.

When I think about preventing conflict, I think about community-building. I am big on self-reflection. When I collaborate with folks for the first time, I like to ask them about their communication preferences and learning styles.

Lynn: I would only add that I think we are best prepared to handle conflict by creating an atmosphere of trust, accountability, and teamwork. Whenever possible, I think it is most effective when employees manage productive relationships and work out issues themselves, but I am available to listen to various perspectives and to provide support for reducing or managing tension. My hope is that this atmosphere provides the needed support when conflict or tension does arise.

We strengthen teamwork through staff meetings in which everyone is encouraged to participate and be heard and through collaborative efforts that deemphasize differences in employee status and value the strengths and interests of each employee.

Do you have any tips for libraries on how not only to recruit but also to retain talented, diverse employees?

Alyssa: Libraries should support professional development opportunities financially, but also generally. For example, our library's dean as well as our Office of Instruction supported our faculty's participation in the Faculty of Color Cross-Institutional Mentorship Program, which was piloted in 2016–17 by Washington's State Board of Community and Technical Colleges and is still running. Seattle Central College also has a women of color affinity group and an Asian/Pacific Islander affinity group that I've attended gatherings for—they were created by the staff and faculty who needed these spaces, and I'm glad there has been no pushback (as far as I know) about the existence of these groups.

Be an ally. I have been in situations where my authority or credibility was being questioned, and my supervisors or coworkers in those instances thankfully were quick to say, "This is Alyssa. She is a faculty member," or "Alyssa's correct. What she described is our policy," or "Alyssa is qualified and capable of handling this problem." Those quick interjections showed that my colleagues noticed the inappropriate behavior/racial microaggression and that they trusted me and had my back.

Lynn: I will add that the institutional work environment should support diversity through its mission statement and throughout its planning and assessment processes. I recommend training that supports diversity work and that articulates the ongoing expectation of exploring the potential racial impact of a given decision, practice, or policy, and asking whose perspective is missing in the process. At the same time, we need to maintain the expectation that white employees take responsibility for understanding and undoing how they benefit from structural racism without placing a disproportionate burden on employees of color to do this work.

How do you recognize and praise and provide feedback to your employees?

Alyssa: For an example, I coordinate our library's Reference Assistant program (the RAs are MLIS candidates at the nearby University of Washington iSchool), and regular opportunities for praise and feedback are built in. I match them with a librarian mentor each quarter so they have the opportunity for structured feedback where they can discuss goal-setting, projects, and reflection. I also check in informally with them about their progress each week.

Our library also has a "Sunshine Committee" that recognizes employee birthdays, celebrates holidays and the end of each quarter, and coordinates cards or care packages for those who are ill or grieving. Even small gestures like these can have an impact on morale and community-building.

Lynn: Individual employees receive feedback through formal evaluation processes. I give employees praise and feedback on a more informal basis as well. Library employees regularly recognize and praise each other through collective e-mail messages, and they share praise at staff meetings.

What specific diversity initiatives are you implementing at Seattle Central College? How do you keep diverse students engaged and excited about library work?

Alyssa: Our library's "Conversations on Social Issues" series has been a successful, long-term weekly event that brings many folks together to engage in discussions about social justice. Guest speakers (students, faculty, staff, community members) lead conversations on topics that interest them or which they have expertise in. Some examples of past topics include Missing & Murdered Indigenous Women, Race & Political Mobilization, and Islamophobia.

Lynn: The library maintains a book display that focuses on topics that highlight the collection and demonstrate the library's attention to different issues and populations. ■ ■ ■

REFERENCES

Cullen, Lisa Takeuchi. 2007. "The Diversity Delusion." *Time*, May 7.

McKenzie, Lindsey. 2017. "The White Face of Library Leadership." August 30. *Inside Higher Ed*. www.insidehighered.com/news/2017/08/30/survey-reveals -overwhelmingly-white-face-leadership-research-libraries.

Newkirk, Pamela. 2019. "Why Diversity Initiatives Fail: Symbolic Gestures and Millions of Dollars Can't Overcome Apathy." November 6. *The Chronicle of Higher Education*, 11, https://www.chronicle.com/article/why-diversity -initiatives-fail/.

Index

ALA TechSource
alatechsource.com

Practical and concise, ALA TechSource publications help you

- Stay on top of emerging technologies
- Discover the latest tools proving effective in libraries
- Implement practical and time-saving strategies
- Learn from industry experts on topics such as privacy policies, online instruction, automation systems, digital preservation, artificial intelligence (AI), and more

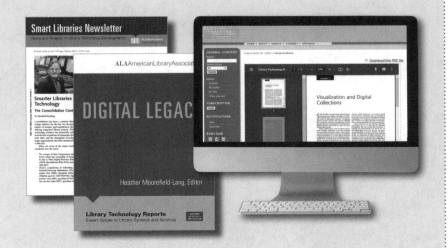